THE VIEW FROM
A MONASTERY

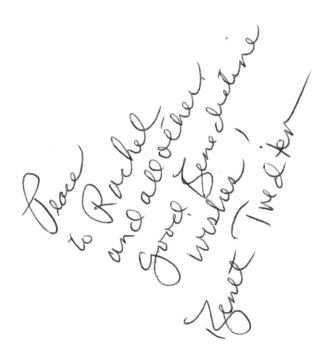

Peace
to Rachel
and all other
good Benedictine
wishes)
Kenneth Tredten

A VOICE FROM THE MONASTERY

THE VIEW

FROM A

MONASTERY

THE VOWED LIFE AND ITS
CAST OF MANY CHARACTERS

Brother Benet Tvedten
NEW FOREWORD BY KATHLEEN NORRIS

PARACLETE PRESS
BREWSTER, MASSACHUSETTS

The View from a Monastery

2006 First Printing This Edition

Copyright © 1999, 2006 by Brother Benet Tvedten

ISBN 10: 1-55725-477-X
ISBN 13: 978-1-55725-477-1

First published in 1999 by Riverhead Books, The Berkley Publishing Group, a division of Penguin Putnam, Inc., New York, New York.

Library of Congress Cataloging-in-Publication data
Tvedten, Benet.
The view from a monastery : the vowed life and its cast of many characters / by Benet Tvedten ; new foreword by Kathleen Norris.—Rev. ed.
  p. cm.
ISBN 1-55725-477-X (trade paper)
1. Monastic and religious life. I. Title.
BX2435.T945 2006
255'.1—dc22   2006016485

The text of the Rule quoted throughout this work is *RB 1980: The Rule of St. Benedict in Latin and English*, edited by Timothy Fry, OSB, © 1981. The quotes from the second book of *The Dialogues of St. Gregory the Great* are from *Life and Miracles of Saint Benedict*, translated by Odo J. Zimmermann, OSB , and Benedict R. Avery, OSB, © 1949 by The Order of Saint Benedict, Inc. Both are published by The Liturgical Press, Collegeville, Minnesota, and are used here with permission.

The title piece was first published in *Dakota Arts Quarterly*, No. 9, Spring 1980 and reprinted in *Inheriting the Land*, edited by Mark Vinz and Thom Tammaro, University of Minnesota Press, 1993. Copyright by Dakota Arts Quarterly. Used with permission.

10 9 8 7 6 5 4 3 2 1

Published by Paraclete Press
Brewster, Massachusetts
www.paracletepress.com

Printed in the United States of America

Dedicated to the monks and oblates of Blue Cloud Abbey

CONTENTS

FOREWORD

Benet Tvedten is a born storyteller, and this book is an invitation to enter the story of a twentieth-century Benedictine monastery and its monks. In a wonderfully hospitable and gentle style, Br. Benet provides the reader not only with a substantial background in monastic history, but makes it clear that this is a living tradition practiced by ordinary men and women. The book also presents a challenge: Those who romanticize monastics as super-holy, perfect people may be disappointed to find that monks don't live up to their standards. And those who regard monks as holier-than-thou anachronisms in today's world may be surprised at the extent to which they identify with these strugglers in the spiritual life. The reader may confidently turn to this book, not for answers, but for nourishment, for stories that can illuminate the path of one's own life.

Benedict makes it clear, at the conclusion to his Rule for monks, that he has written a rule for beginners. He insists that a holy life begins where we are, not where we wish, or imagine ourselves, to be. The Rule is not given to discussions of theology, arcane knowledge concerning the true nature of

God, or the depths of spiritual insight that a monk might attain. Rather, it focuses on the daily chores and routine personal interactions of life. And it is here that we discover the radical asceticism that Benedict had in mind. Stop for a moment and think about your church, the business at which you work, or the school you attend. Imagine that you must not only work with the people there, but pray, eat, and take your recreation with them as well. Now imagine that you have promised to do this for the rest of your life. This is the vow that Benedictines take, praying that God will not disappoint them in their hope that somehow they will learn to love these peculiar and difficult neighbors as they love themselves.

This brief book is rich with stories of how monks come to love Christ, and others, through visits to the dentist and communal movie-viewing, through tending to each other in bouts of illness or in struggles with alcoholism and depression. It would be all too easy to relegate monks to museums, or to see them as part of a golden past in which it was easier to lead a pure and holy life. But as Br. Benet's many citations from earlier monastic literature indicate, there never was such a past. Monks have always squabbled about how much wine they're allowed to have with meals, and what form of authority should be granted to community leaders. While monastic life is solidly grounded on such essentials as praying the psalms and bearing with each other's weaknesses in the love of Christ, it has always been experimental, always subject to revision. As Br. Benet suggests, it is the willingness of monks to live through this tension between flexibility and stability that has allowed the tradition to survive for over 1,500 years, in the Egyptian desert, in the great cities of Europe, and in a rural enclave of eastern South Dakota.

–Kathleen Norris
April 2006

ACKNOWLEDGMENTS

Thanks to everyone at Paraclete Press for considering this book worthy of a new edition. I'm grateful for the opportunity to work with Lil Copan, Jon Sweeney, Robert Edmonson, Sister Mercy Minor, Danielle Bushnell, and Pamela Jordan. All of you have shared the view from my monastery.

The table then spoke of Mount Melleray, how bracing the air was down there, how hospitable the monks were, and how they never asked for a penny-piece from their guests.
"And do you mean to say, " asked Mr. Browne incredulously, "that a chap can go down there and put up there as if it were a hotel and live on the fat of the land and then come away without paying anything?"
—from *The Dead*, by James Joyce

"They are very good men, the monks, very pious men. "
—from the same

THE VIEW FROM

A MONASTERY

The View From a Monastery

I n the northeastern corner of South Dakota where I live,
there are two attractions to which sightseers are drawn: a
cheese factory and a monastery. The monastery is located
two hundred miles west of Minneapolis and one hundred
thirty miles from both Fargo and Sioux Falls, the two largest
cities in the Dakotas. A sign at a roadside park on U.S.
Highway 12 indicates that the monastery is one of the nearby
points of interest, and motorists who pass through frequently
swing by for a look. On Sunday afternoons, people who live
in the area like to drive out to see the monastery. During the
week, a busload of people might arrive, bearing a homemakers'
club, school children, or a group of senior citizens.
Sometimes they have come directly to the monastery from
the cheese factory.

I have lived in the monastery for over forty years, and I
have witnessed this unending stream of tourists. Neighbors
of the monastery often like to bring visiting relatives and
friends here for a tour. One day people from Kansas,
Wisconsin, Florida, California, and Norway signed the guest
register. On occasion, I have had the responsibility of showing
the monastery to people who have arranged a tour. Many of

them appear genuinely impressed by what they see. Others are obviously baffled. This is understandable, because monasticism will always be a mystery to most people. Some tourists are concerned only about the physical structure of the place. They compliment us for having constructed the monastery ourselves and seldom ask about our prayer life.

There are many false notions about monasticism. Pious people think that monks are holy. People who don't know much about religion think we are peculiar. The truth of the matter is that we are neither, though I have known individual monks who were both. Most of us are ordinary men who find that it is easier for us to be holier here than in some other place.

Brother Patrick was holy. His holiness was not the kind that is commonly associated with sanctity, but he was my kind of saint. He was not a plaster saint. He had a solid piety without being the least bit sanctimonious. Ambrose Bierce, the nineteenth-century American writer, said, "A saint is a dead sinner, revised and edited." I prefer remembering Brother Patrick in all of his originality. He came to the monastery when he was in his fifties and lived with us for fifteen years. On his deathbed, he told us that the happiest years of his life had been spent in the monastery. Earlier he had worked on the General Motors assembly line in Flint, Michigan, and before that he had fought in the Battle of the Bulge. If we had been naive, we would have been convinced from his tales that he had won this decisive battle of World War II single-handedly.

Brother Paddy worked in our laundry for a while. By the time we had grown accustomed to pranks like having our underwear starched, he was transferred to the monastery kitchen. His menus were posted so that we could always be prepared. We learned not to expect much for lunch on "T.T.

and R." day. No one was ever able to establish whether "Turkey Turds and Rainwater" was an army term or if Brother Paddy had invented it himself. The other veterans in the monastery claimed never to have heard the expression. Paddy had been on the winning side in the Battle of the Bulge, and in more recent years he had won his own personal battle with alcoholism. Now, however, he knew that cancer would win the last battle. He'd had two skirmishes with it. This time it was inoperable.

A week before his death, he was as eager as ever to entertain all of the "brethren" (as he called us) who gathered at his bedside. Sitting on the edge of his bed and chain-smoking cigarettes ("Why not? I don't have lung cancer"), he regaled us with war stories and recollections of his youth in an upstate New York town where he could buy a bucket of beer for a nickel. When Brother James was alone with him one day, Brother Paddy told him, "Jim, when you see that I'm gone, grab this watch off my wrist. Don't let any of the brethren get to it first. It's a good watch, and it'll keep time for you the rest of your life."

A day or so before he lost consciousness, he told those of us who were in his smoke-filled room, "I hope you bastards have to bury me on the coldest day of the winter." We could have pleaded with him to wait for spring, but he was ready to leave and he seemed assured of his destination. We carried Brother Patrick to the monastery cemetery not on the coldest day of that winter but on a day with a wind-chill factor that would nevertheless have pleased him.

There is some misunderstanding about where monks come from, a notion that we are conditioned from childhood to enter a monastery, or that our previous circumstances in life were different from other people's. This is not so. We had other alternatives. One monk gave up a navy career. Another abandoned his studies for a doctorate. Others had to dispose of a farm or a business.

Some of us came to the monastery from cities—Milwaukee, Seattle, Indianapolis, Minneapolis—and others came from farms and small towns in the Dakotas. Why did we leave and come to this place? I know when I look down into the valley at night. The monastery is built on a rise from which the flat farmland of the Whetstone Valley can be seen. In the dark, the fields are not visible, but the lights are. The lights from Ortonville, thirty miles away in Minnesota, the lights from Milbank, half that distance, and the lights of the smaller towns—Wilmot, Corona, Twin Brooks—all these lights and the yard lights on the farms create an illusion. I look at the valley and I think that I see an enormous city. It is distant and I am removed from it. This is the way it should be, I tell myself.

This is the way it was in the third and fourth centuries when throngs of Christians fled from the cities and went to live in the desert. They believed the *parousia* (the second coming of Christ) was imminent. They wanted to be ready. In the desert, apart from the rest of mankind, these hermits could prepare themselves by prayer and penance. The word "monk" comes from the Greek *monos*, meaning alone, solitary. Gradually, these hermit-monks evolved into communities. The *parousia* didn't occur, but monasticism became firmly rooted in Christendom. *Fuga munda*—flight from the world—is no longer a retreat to the desert, but men still seek to live apart from the rest of society in monasteries such as ours. Although we can hear the muffled sounds of traffic along U.S. Highway 12, there is an appreciable sense of solitude on our hill.

Near the end of the fifth century, St. Benedict, the Father of Western Monasticism, abandoned his studies in the city of

Rome and went to live in a cave. I can understand why St. Benedict left the city. Sometimes when I look at the lights in the valley, I think of the things I'd like to do in that imaginary city. Most of the time, though, I am satisfied to be where I am. And at dawn when we are on our way to morning prayer, and the lights in the valley are going off and the sun is rising, then I can see reality—hay bales and fields of corn and alfalfa. It is much better for a monk to live in the country. Agrarians can understand our need to work the land, to grow much of our own food, to provide bread for both the table and the altar. People who are into Zen and Transcendental Meditation can appreciate our need for contemplation. Communitarians know how important it is for us to depend on the resources of those with whom we share our lot. We hold all things in common, and the whole community benefits, directly or indirectly, from the abilities of the individual monks—the teacher, the carpenter, the potter, the beekeeper, the weaver, the priest, even the writer. People who come here to make a retreat, to absorb the atmosphere of the monastery, know what we are about. Still, there are countless others for whom we remain mysterious.

Between the monastery church and the Whetstone Valley is the cemetery. The trees surrounding the cemetery are obscured by the night. In the moonlight, I cannot distinguish a Russian olive from a spruce, but I know the trees are there and I know that they enclose the graves of monks. There is no illusion here. This is where our bodies wait for their resurrection. You see, monks still believe that the *parousia* will happen. This is why we came to the monastery, and, perhaps, this is why we will always remain an enigma to many people.

🌿 St. Benedict and His Rule

It was impossible for St. Benedict to flee from the world. In the ages before his, other hermits also had a hard time escaping. They were driven deeper and deeper into the desert by the curious who kept seeking them out. Not everyone who found the hermit's hiding place came to gawk, however. Some people sought him out because of a desire to have him impart wisdom to them.

St. Benedict left his cave because monks nearby wanted him for their abbot. They soon changed their minds about that and tried to kill him. After refusing to accept the reforms of monastic observance proposed by St. Benedict, these monks tried poisoning his drink—but the glass pitcher that contained it broke when he blessed the wine at table. "Go and find yourselves an abbot to your liking," he told the monks. "It is impossible for me to stay here any longer." He returned to the cave at Subiaco and established monastic life there. Later he and some of his monks moved to Monte Cassino, where he wrote the Rule. The Rule was written for monks, but nuns also accepted it as their guide for Christian living. At the time of St. Benedict's death in 547, the Rule was followed in only a few monasteries in central Italy. By the ninth century, it had supplanted many other monastic rules. By the twelfth century, it had become the universal rule of monks and nuns. St. Benedict was a wise abbot. He was flexible and moderate. This is why the Rule has lasted all these centuries. Although many of its regulations are no longer practical or practiced, the basic principles of the Rule have remained the same. Some of the customs that existed when I became a monk were accretions from the late Middle Ages. One of these was the manner in which we showed respect for the abbot. In those days when he was the celebrant of Mass, we had to kiss his ring, a symbol of abbatial authority, before receiving communion. This ritual often confused newcomers to the monastery. The abbot sometimes suffered the displeasure of having the stone in his ring licked by the communicant whose tongue was ready to receive the host but who had forgotten to kiss the ring first. We no longer have to do this, nor do we kneel and kiss the abbot's ring when we enter or leave his office. Our present abbot doesn't even wear a ring. St. Benedict would not have been comfortable with many of the trappings that accrued to the abbot over the years. He would have found them pretentious. In the Rule, he said an abbot should not seek "preeminence for himself" (64:8).

The Second Vatican Council, which was convened by Pope John XXIII, met in Rome between 1962 and 1965 in order to modernize and revitalize the Catholic Church. *Aggiornamento* was the Italian word the Pope used for this updating. Among the decrees promulgated by the Council Fathers was one that called for "The Appropriate Renewal of the Religious Life." In this document, members of religious orders were advised to recapture the spirit of their founders. Although the spirit of St. Benedict is clearly manifested in his Rule, we found ourselves responding to surveys and questionnaires. Community meetings were held so frequently in the 1960s that our abbot quipped, "Nowadays, monks profess the vows of poverty, chastity, and discussion." Besides returning to the spirit of our founder, we were expected to update ourselves. Obsolete customs were discarded and adaptations were made in various areas. The most radical change was in the manner of worship when modern English replaced ancient Latin.

Perhaps some religious orders were baffled by the decree from Rome. They may have asked themselves: What if the spirit of our founder has nothing to do with the spirit of the times? We Benedictines had the evidence of history that the Rule of our Holy Patriarch had been an effective guide for generations of monks and nuns. Returning to the spirit of our founder was a matter of asking ourselves how we had departed from the Rule of St. Benedict. Kissing the abbot's ring seemed to be one of the things that were not in accord with St. Benedict's teachings.

The Rule indicates what St. Benedict disliked: grumbling, laziness, wastefulness, indifference, and arrogance. And what he liked: a sense of responsibility, honesty, temperance, and simplicity. He gave us a regulated life. He had us profess a vow of stability.

Living under the Rule is supposed to make us face reality and stop thinking about what might have been or what life might be like now in different circumstances. This is what we mean by stability. All of us who follow the Rule of St. Benedict learn to live one day at a time. The Rule of St. Benedict is basically a document of daily routine, a blueprint for people who live together day after day. It teaches us to settle down. "They no longer live by their own judgment, giving in to their whims and appetites; rather they walk according to another's decisions and directions, choosing to live in monasteries and to have an abbot over them" (5:12).

St. Benedict ends the Rule by declaring that anyone who follows it will achieve "some degree of virtue" (73:1). He doesn't promise perfection. He doesn't even expect it. Sometimes, applicants to the monastery make a point of telling the vocation director how very good they've always been and still are. We prefer hearing from people who tell us they aren't perfect. They have a better chance of fitting into the community. St. Benedict does not demand heroic virtue. Nor are hair shirts and chains to be found in our wardrobes. No extraordinary means are to be taken in procuring and preserving virtue. A prospective candidate for our monastery once asked me, "Do you use the discipline?" He appeared disappointed when I told him we don't whip our bodies. If such a practice was once fashionable in religious orders, it was never a custom in ours. St. Benedict would have frowned upon anything masochistic. He cautions us to be practical, even about the season of Lent. Don't presume to do more penance than is good for you, he says.

How the Monastery Came to Be Here

A retired rural mail carrier living in Marvin, the little town a mile from our abbey, told the founding monks that he had once lived on the property that is now ours. He had a relative, a Benedictine nun, who used to visit him and his wife those many years ago. The nun had the custom of burying medals of St. Benedict in the soil, beseeching his protection of garden and fields. In 1949, when the monks of St. Benedict came from Indiana to look for a site on which to build this monastery, late autumn's sun setting over these Coteau Hills overwhelmed them. They stopped at a farm and asked about the availability of land in the area. The farmer directed them to one of the banks in Milbank, the county seat. The man at the bank said, "Yes, I know that part of the country. Just a few minutes ago someone from out there was in here to arrange the selling of a farm. Maybe you will want to buy it." The man who offered this valuable information was named Mr. Benedict. The farm he had in mind was the one where the medals of St. Benedict had been buried in the ground. These are the legends we tell about our founding.

This is the story told by the monk who purchased our property at the public auction and who, along with volunteer workmen, was responsible for preparing the deserted farm buildings for occupancy: "I said the first Mass in the house on the kitchen sink, using an old shed door for the altar top. Then I rigged up that chicken house and said Mass in it every day thereafter. The mice used to run across the altar while I was saying Mass. It rained one day, and there was a hole in the center of the house where the brooder stovepipe used to go through. When I turned around for the *Dominus vobiscum*, my faithful workers were seen through a shower. The dormitory room was a sheep stable, and we shoveled a foot and a half of organic matter out of it."

Some of the townspeople were alarmed when they heard that monks were moving into the neighborhood. How would you feel about having a monastery planted in your backyard? The retired mail carrier and his wife and another elderly couple were the town's only Catholics. Everyone got along well with them and they with the town's Lutherans and Baptists. But here was a whole horde of papists moving in— and the strangest kind. Monks! No wonder there was cause for concern. Martians might just as well have been descending on them.

A town meeting was called. Fortunately, one of the townspeople stood in our defense. He said, "They aren't even here yet and you've already condemned them. Give the bastards a chance." It didn't take long for our neighbors to realize we meant them no harm. We became good friends and have remained so. They affectionately call us "The Abbey Boys." If you aren't from around here, you might think that's the name of a country-western band.

 *Legends*

From the time I entered the novitiate and learned about my Benedictine forebears until now, Pope St. Gregory the Great was presumed to have written the biography of St. Benedict in the summer of 593. This was less than fifty years after St. Benedict's death. Now there is some doubt among scholars about Gregory's authorship and when exactly the biography was written. The author, whether or not he was a scribe in the Vatican Library almost a hundred years later, has given us wonderful legends of a saint. Until there is a consensus, however, I prefer identifying Gregory as the biographer of Benedict.

In every monastery there are monks who show their potential for becoming legendary characters. We recognize them while they are still with us, and when they are gone we tell stories about them and make certain that our memory of them never diminishes. Oral tradition is very important in monasteries. The stories are family heirlooms, which are passed on from one generation to another.

Whenever I visit other monasteries, my hosts reminisce about memorable characters in their communities. They tell the kinds of stories that are so often repeated in my own monastic family. "Now, do you remember the time Father Dan got the car stuck in the mud? There was a horse in the pasture next to the road. Father Dan got the horse and tied its tail to the front bumper of the car. Then he got behind the steering wheel and leaned on the horn. The horse bolted and ran off, leaving most of the hair from its tail on the bumper."

This incident with the horse is one of the anecdotes that will be told about Father Dan for many years to come. I've heard several versions of the story. In one, the tail itself was left attached to the bumper. We could have asked Father Dan to tell us once again the exact circumstances, but it wouldn't have mattered. The story had already become a legend, and each of us tells it his own way.

The life of St. Benedict is filled with stories, many of them having to do with miracles wrought by the Abbot of Monte Cassino for the benefit of his monks and for people in the neighborhood. They are contained in what has been known as Book Two of *The Dialogues of St. Gregory the Great*. He relates all of these legends to an imaginary character named Deacon Peter. "I should like to tell you much more about this saintly abbot," Gregory says, "but I am purposely passing over some of his miraculous deeds in my eagerness to take up others." Before going on to relate the more pertinent stories, Gregory tells Peter, "With all the renown he gained by his numerous miracles, the holy man was no less outstanding for the wisdom of his teaching. He wrote a rule for monks that is remarkable for its discretion and its clarity of language. Anyone who wishes to know more about his life and character can discover in his Rule exactly what he was like as an abbot, for his life could not have differed from his teaching."

Just as there is conjecture nowadays regarding the author of St. Benedict's life, so was there once controversy regarding the legislator of his Rule. When I was a novice forty-some years ago, I never heard about the Rule of the Master. Although scholars were discussing it, this was no time to tell novices that St. Benedict had borrowed from someone else in the composition of his Rule. Nowadays, everyone agrees that St. Benedict condensed the Rule of the Master, which was written in the vicinity of Rome at the end of the fifth century. St. Benedict threw out whole chapters and changed the tone of others. He would not rule a monastery in the same manner the anonymous Master did. St. Benedict says an abbot should not be "excitable, anxious, extreme, obstinate, jealous, or over suspicious." The Master has all of these unfavorable characteristics. He had very little discretion.

Indeed, we can learn much about St. Benedict from the Rule as it has been passed on through the generations of monastic men and women.

How I Came to Be Here

As a teenager in a small North Dakota town, I read Thomas Merton's autobiography *The Seven Storey Mountain.* The description on the book's jacket informed me this was the story of "a young man who lived an exciting worldly life until the age of twenty-six, when he entered a Trappist monastery." This meant that Merton got drunk, read dirty books, and flirted with Communism before becoming a monk. At least this was how I, a high-school sophomore, interpreted his "exciting worldly life."

It was Merton's book that first prompted my interest in monasticism. At that age, though, I was more interested in the theater. Every month when I went to the orthodontist in Fargo, I stopped at the newsstand in the bus depot and bought a copy of *Theatre Arts.* There were never more than two copies of the magazine on the rack. I daydreamed about being an actor, but I revealed this aspiration to no one. I was afraid of being told that membership in the drama club was all right in high school, but one simply didn't make it a profession—not even if one's crooked teeth had been straightened.

Since becoming a monk, I've met several others of my profession who have acknowledged Merton's influence in either drawing them to the monastic life or in keeping them there once they arrived. Merton belonged to the Trappists, a religious order that places great emphasis on silence. Out of this silence came words. He was a silent monk who dared to speak out in prose and poetry. He was an apologist of the monastic tradition, but he also became a prophet calling for change within the monastic order. When I was still in high school, a young man from my hometown joined the Trappists and came back a few years later terribly emaciated and with his head shaved. I remember wondering why Merton's kind of monasticism had to be so rough on people.

In college at St. John's in Minnesota I encountered monks of another kind. Most of my professors were Benedictines, and their life appeared to be less penitential than that of the Trappists. By now, I knew something about monastic history. The Trappists were reformed Cistercians who were reformed Benedictines. All three orders followed the Rule of St. Benedict. The two reform movements occurred when it was believed that the Rule was no longer being observed as St. Benedict would have wished. But it was clear to me that the Benedictines lived by the spirit of the Rule if not by the letter of the law.

On the day my parents took me to college, from the moment I saw two black-robed, hooded monks strolling on the road leading to their community's institution of higher learning, I fell in love with the Benedictines. I became a monk watcher. Some of the monks were friendly; others were aloof. Some were docile, and others were easily perturbed. Another freshman told me he'd heard of one who had become so upset by the ignorance of his students that he threw an eraser at them, shouting, "I'd give up if I didn't love you goddamned sons of bitches." To me, monks seemed pretty much like ordinary people.

While pursuing a degree in English, I had it in the back of my mind that I would become a monk someday. There were two distinct classes in monastic life then: priests and brothers. I was attracted to the latter because I had no desire to seek ordination. Besides, the brothers appeared more genuinely monastic. In its origins, monasticism was a lay movement. St. Benedict himself was not a priest. Although he foresaw the need for an abbot to choose one of his monks for ordination, it was by way of exception that someone who was already an ordained priest was accepted into the monastery. St. Benedict was fearful that such a person would be lacking in humility and would become demanding because of his priestly status.

I soon learned, however, that the brothers were treated as second-class citizens in the monastery. They were forbidden by church law to hold certain offices, they could not vote on matters affecting the whole community, and they were restricted in the kinds of work they could do. St. Benedict would have been disqualified from being an abbot in a twentieth-century monastery because he was not a priest. Monasticism had departed from his idea of a classless society with equal rights.

Nevertheless, I felt comfortable with the Benedictines. And in a few years, changes would take place in monasticism. Many of the former distinctions between ordained and non-ordained monks would disappear after Vatican II. This was certainly evident at my alma mater when a brother was named president of the college.

Monks of the monastery I entered, in addition to inhabiting the monastery itself, were living among Native American people on four reservations in the Dakotas. Most of them had been assigned to these missions while they were still members of St. Meinrad's Abbey in Indiana. When Blue Cloud Abbey was founded, it took on the responsibility of staffing the missions. The new monastery was named in memory of Mahpiyato, a tribal leader who was buried at the mission on the Yankton Reservation in South Dakota. Beginning in 1970, we initiated a policy of transferring the mission schools to the ownership and administration of the local tribes. Monks remained on the reservations for another twenty years, tending to the pastoral needs of the Dakota and Ojibwa people. Then we withdrew from this ministry altogether.

Although I was aware of the monastery's involvement in the missions, I was attracted to Blue Cloud Abbey's monastic life because there was more democracy here than elsewhere. Unlike the custom at other monasteries, including St. Meinrad's, there was no separation between the priests and brothers. They mingled during work and recreation. Fraternization between priests and brothers was not only tolerated here, it was encouraged. There were no separate novitiates for clerical and non-clerical novices. There was only one novitiate class and one novice master. I was convinced that I'd found the type of monastery St. Benedict would have found praiseworthy.

George, my college friend from South Dakota, first told me about the monastery. When he entered the novitiate here, I attended his investiture ceremony. When I applied for entrance two years later, George was no longer here. He almost returned the year I made first vows, but he changed his mind and went out West. He's disappeared from my life but not my memory.

The youngest of three sons, I was born late in my parents' marriage. As an adult, I learned it had been feared that my mother might not survive my birth. If this had been the case, my three maiden Lutheran aunts would have helped raise me.

Ole Tvedten, their brother and my father, was a Norwegian who had married Margaret Rose O'Neill in the parish rectory instead of the sanctuary of the parish church because he was not a Catholic.

Although he eventually converted to Catholicism, my mother bore the greater influence in raising the three of us in the faith of her ancestors. "Would you ever skip church on a Sunday?" an exasperated nephew asked me when his father, brother, and I were traveling together. All morning we kept pulling off the Interstate, looking for a Catholic church where Mass was about to begin.

"Not deliberately," I said.

"All this fuss is because of the Irish mother you guys had."

I think he was correct in his assertion. We learned from our mother that Catholics are obliged to attend Sunday Mass, but I agreed that this search for one was frustrating.

My two brothers were heading off for World War II when I began school. Although I had no siblings in the house, I had friends of my age in the neighborhood. On Saturdays, the nuns came out from Fargo to teach us Catholic children the catechism. I suppose it was from one of them that I was taught that Jesus Christ was the founder of the Catholic Church, and Martin Luther was the founder of the one named after him. I never felt superior to my Lutheran friends, and I was convinced that they, like my own Lutheran relatives, were just as worthy of attaining heaven as the Catholics. After all, I'd heard the Lutheran kids sing, "Jesus loves me. This I know. For the Bible tells me so." When I got to college, the Benedictines introduced me to reading the Bible, which I discovered was not an exclusively Protestant book.

My parents cried the day I kissed them good-bye and left home for the monastery. Three months later, they cried again when they visited me for the first time. An old Irish aunt was with them. They arrived just as Mass was beginning, and I couldn't greet them until afterward. When I approached them in the garb of a candidate—the tunic and scapular without a hood—their tears poured forth.

"Why are you crying?" I asked, knowing it was at the sight of my changed appearance. I'm sure it didn't help that my head, like those of the other candidates and novices, had been shaved in order to keep us from being vain.

It was November 2, 1958, All Souls' Day, on which deceased loved ones are commemorated. My parents told me they were crying because the sermon was so sad.

The following month, it was my turn to cry. On Christmas night, I put on my parka and went outdoors so no one could see me. This was my first Christmas away from home, and I missed my parents and my brothers and their families. Everyone was at home for the holiday, but I couldn't be with them. Get used to it, I told myself. From now on this is your home. Then I cried some more.

High Liturgy/Low Liturgy

Most of us, when asked why we entered the monastery, will readily answer that we were called by God. The inquirer may want to know if there was one particular moment when this call was clearly manifested. I don't think I had a mystical revelation. But I do remember that the first time I heard the monks singing Gregorian chant at St. John's Abbey, I had something akin to an out-of-the-body experience.

Some people are attracted to the externals of monasticism rather than by its essence. When I was a novice, I sometimes wondered if this hadn't been the case for me.

Was I enamored with the monastic life because of my love for the theater? The solemn liturgical celebrations were great performances acted out in exquisite vesture: At a pontifical High Mass, the abbot wore his precious miter—a pointed hat studded with jewels. I especially liked the vestments—worn by the abbot, the assistant priest, deacon, and subdeacon—that had decorative designs sewn on them with gold thread. There were various minor parts to be played in these liturgies, and the candidates and novices were cast in them. We wore white gloves and long surplices over our habits. The stage directions called for a lot of bowing and lots of incensing.

But all of this was for feast days only. The grand liturgical productions didn't have long runs. I soon learned that the essence of monasticism is living the day-by-day routine—the seeking of God in what is ordinary.

During the novitiate, we had to sit through an hour-long chant class every Friday afternoon. This was not an out-of-the-body experience by any means. I found it a bodily burden.

Bruder Felix

"The monks are doing all the work themselves. This method avoids strikes and other labor problems" That's what the Abbot of St. Meinrad's said about his community's establishment in South Dakota. I knew I was taking a risk when I entered the monastery during its construction era. The monks were also taking a risk in accepting me. I had never pushed a buggy of cement up a ramp or driven a nail into a form or unloaded a steel beam from a truck. I had come to the monastery from my father's grocery store, where I had been a clerk and stocker of shelves, not a construction worker. On the evening of my arrival at the monastery, I went for a walk with one of the monks and expressed to him my worry about the kind of employment I'd be given. He agreed there wasn't much besides construction work for me to do. "The farm, maybe?" God, no!

In the morning, I was assigned to washing windows in the recently completed guest wing. I fell out of the first window I washed and broke five bones in my left foot. When I came home from the hospital, I was wearing a cast up to my knee. Now it was impossible for the monks to give me a job in construction, so I was sent to the appeal office, where I typed envelopes and recorded donations. Although our mother abbey was providing us with sandstone quarried from its Indiana ground, we still had to solicit funds for other building materials.

My desk and Father Lawrence's were at one end of the room and Brother Felix was at the opposite end with his addressing machine and name plates. There seemed to be an invisible wall between us. In later years, some of the monks called it "The Berlin Wall." No one dared enter that restricted area without Brother Felix's authorization. He kept wrapping paper, manila envelopes, rubber bands, and other supplies there. If anyone was foolish enough to help himself to any of these items without Brother Felix's permission, the penalty for being apprehended in the act was a severe reprimand.

Although Brother Felix was a naturalized citizen of the United States and had lived in this country for over sixty years, he constantly reminded us that he was a German by birth and at heart. He once told a confrere, "I'm not like you. I had clothes on when I came to this country." In his youth, he had learned the printer's trade. While a candidate at Kloster Andechs in Bavaria, he decided to pursue his Benedictine vocation in the United States rather than in Germany. He was one of several brother-monks recruited from Germany after the First World War because of the scarcity of vocations to the brotherhood in Indiana.

Monks from Einsiedeln Abbey, in Switzerland, founded St. Meinrad's in 1854. When they came to the New World, the monks settled in an area populated by German-speaking immigrants. The sons of these people entered the monastery in its early years. Until vocations began arriving from other ethnic groups, German was the language of the house. There was still a vestige of it in 1934 when our Father Brendan entered St. Meinrad's Abbey. The son of Irish immigrants, he'd had to learn German in order to be a reader during meals in the monastery refectory.

Young men from a Germany devastated by war must have welcomed the opportunity to come to this country in the 1920s. Most of them were skilled in various arts and crafts. When an increase of American-born vocations to the brotherhood occurred in the following decades, another distinction—besides the one between brothers and priests— arose in the monastery. Outside of work hours, the two groups lived separate lives. A member of our community, recalling his days as a young brother at St. Meinrad's, says, "The Germans thought we Americans were soft and lazy."

Brother Felix never lost his love for the *Vaterland*. His first trip back to Germany was in 1936 for the ordination of his brother, a Capuchin friar. All religious processions had been banned in the town of Turkheim, but the Haug family wanted to process from their home to the parish church where Father Fortis would offer his first Mass.

Their relative from America went to the local head of the Nazi Party and informed him there would be a procession. And there was.

Brother Felix called the rest of us "you Americans." He often told us, "You Americans drink your beer too cold." He claimed that Germans drink their beer at room temperature. He drank our beer, but it was not as good as German beer. The best beer in all of Europe, he said, was brewed at Andechs, the monastery where he had been a candidate. When Father Damien was touring Europe, he stopped at Andechs and tasted the beer. He had to admit that Brother Felix had sacrificed one of the great pleasures in life when he immigrated to the United States.

Brother Felix thought Americans were inept in many other ways as well. One day when he was scolding a fellow monk for some impropriety, the monk ingeniously distracted him by asking, "Is it true that trains run on time in Germany?" The issue at hand was dropped immediately, and Brother Felix began praising the German railroad system over our inferior one.

He held strong opinions about almost everything. There were certain subjects we avoided mentioning in his presence. He disliked changes and he resisted most of them. He often told us, "You do what you want to do, and I'll do what I want to do." He adhered to whatever was familiar to him, to whatever suited him. Until his dying day, he followed the Mass with his old *St. Andrew's Daily Missal*, and he observed all the former rubrics in the Mass that had been changed or abolished in the 1960s. While the rest of us were singing "Holy, Holy, Holy," he could be heard whispering *"Sanctus, Sanctus, Sanctus."* As his hearing diminished, his Latin became louder and louder. He detested the use of the guitar in our liturgies, and although he had Protestant friends, he saw no need to sing their hymns in our church. He plugged his ears with his fingers whenever we sang "A Mighty Fortress Is Our God."

He was the sacristan for a number of years. No priest ever went unto the altar of God without first passing Brother Felix's inspection. When priests were in the sacristy vesting for their private Masses, the sacristan would make the rounds, pulling, tugging, and yanking on albs, amices, and chasubles.

For thirty-five years Brother Felix conscientiously answered our telephone and carried our personal mail to and from the Marvin Post Office. He checked every envelope to make sure the correct Zip Code was being used. If an error had been made, he would correct both the envelope and the sender. He would even track down guests to inform them of their mistakes. He insisted that things be done the right way. That meant his way. With regard to the mail, though, he told us, "This is not my idea. It is postal regulation." We took it for granted that he was correct. We even allowed him to trim off the margins of overweight letters in order to save postage. We also took it for granted that he would always answer the telephone. If another monk did answer the phone and was caught doing so, Brother Felix would tell him, "Get off the phone. That's my job." Some monks were afraid to answer the telephone even when Brother Felix was in Germany visiting relatives.

Although Brother Felix had a temper that could be easily aroused, he was quick to make amends. He seldom said, "I'm sorry," but atonement was made through little gifts and unsought favors. Ordinarily he was friendly and jovial. *Gemutlich*. He had friends all over the countryside. Many of them attended his funeral, which was one of the largest ever held in our community. In his twilight years, he made several trips back to Germany. The last time he went home, he celebrated his eightieth birthday in the house where he was born. Brother Felix went his own way most of the time, but he never strayed away from us. He also loved his finches and spoke and sang to them all day long. Sometimes he played phonograph records for them of German polkas. They responded with their own kind of music. After saying good night to his finches one All Hallows' Eve, he covered their cages and then went to bed himself, and died. So did one of his finches the same night.

The Brother Instructor

Father Gualbert had never been stationed on an Indian reservation, but in 1948 he was named superior of St. Paul's Mission at Marty, South Dakota. It was rumored that he was the recently deceased superior's choice to succeed him. Another rumor was that Father Sylvester's death was a fortuitous occasion for ridding St. Meinrad's Abbey of a troublemaker.

In the beginning, Father Gualbert had been placed over the brothers who had not made final vows. He upgraded their monastic life, often in the midst of controversy. The junior brothers were all American-born, and Father Gualbert believed their needs differed from those of the older German brothers. He improved their physical surroundings by having the junior brothers paint the walls in their living quarters. He converted an area below the library into an oratory. Here the junior brothers began praying in English the monastic Divine Office. This replaced the Little Office of the Blessed Virgin Mary that the old brothers continued using. Brother Felix prayed it all his life. Besides improving the quality of the younger brothers' spiritual life, Father Gualbert also sought to develop their intellects. He began a study club in which books were discussed and papers presented by the brothers. In 1942, the junior brothers initiated *Vox Pacis*, a publication featuring poetry, essays, and news items written by the brothers. A young American brother of this era had a clerical job, and a visitor to the abbey was amazed when she saw him typing. He said, "Not only can I type, I can read and write too."

By 1945, distinctions between the two groups began disappearing, and Father Gualbert was named superior of all brothers, regardless of their age or ethnic origins. The older brothers, however, continued to recreate separately. As death took its toll among them, the praying of the Little Office in common ceased, and the survivors said it privately. Earlier tensions began to diminish as the number of American vocations to the brotherhood increased and the Germans became a minority.

Father Gualbert's piety was solidly liturgical. He wanted to see the liturgy rendered in an appropriate manner, and he took care that liturgical furnishings were of artistic quality. Long before the liturgical changes of Vatican II in the 1960s, Father Gualbert wanted to erect the altar in the junior brothers' oratory so that mass could be offered facing them. There was opposition from within the community. Permission was refused. Such a practice was simply not allowed in those days. He got around the objections by situating the altar several feet away from the wall and running the choir stalls all the way to the wall. Standing on his side of the altar, most of the brothers were able to attend the Eucharist with the priest facing them. In 1946, after much discussion in the monastery, all of the brothers were allowed to attend Mass with the rest of the community every day of the week instead of Sundays and holy days only.

Hands Under the Scapular, Please

When I was newly come to the monastic life, one of the first things I learned was the proper decorum for choir. By choir I mean the community assembled for prayer, or the Divine Office. We walked in procession into church two by two, with our hands concealed under the scapular of our habits. Bowing to the crucifix over the altar and then to his partner, each monk went to his assigned choir stall in order of seniority. If we made a mistake in the recitation or singing of the psalms, we bowed an apology to the crucifix. At the end of every psalm, we stood and bowed for the doxology in reverence for the Father, Son, and Holy Spirit. If a monk crossed his legs in choir, he was quickly corrected. That was not proper decorum. If a serious mistake was made in the Divine Office, one that disrupted the whole choir, the monk or monks responsible had to kneel in the middle of choir in reparation. If a monk arrived late for Divine Office, he had to kneel in the middle of choir before going to his place. Latecomers always had to take the last place, no matter what their seniority. This was serious business and it still is, but we get by with less bowing nowadays.

Once a novice got the giggles at Divine Office, and when the novice master tried restraining him, he got the giggles too. Both of them were ordered out because they lacked discipline. The prior was responsible for maintaining discipline in the monastery, and we had a prior who excelled in his craft. Once—just once—I cheerfully greeted him on the stairway. He glared at me when I said, "Good afternoon, Father Prior." I was breaking day silence. No unnecessary speech was allowed during the day. Father Prior Meinrad's glare was not exactly malevolent, but it was foreboding enough to convince me of dire consequences.

Father Meinrad's life was disciplined, and he expected the same kind of self-control from the other monks. He exercised physical discipline as well as the discipline of monastic observance. Every summer he swam and took long hikes. Monks sometimes discovered him splitting logs in the ravine, his habit off, wearing nothing but his union suit.

He died of injuries sustained in a car accident on his way to the clinic, where he was going to be tested for a hearing aid. He'd missed his nap after lunch because of the appointment, and it was presumed he'd fallen asleep at the wheel. In order to prevent other accidents like Father Meinrad's, we began purchasing cars equipped with radios. Father Meinrad, however, would never have listened to a radio in order to combat drowsiness—not even with the benefit of a new hearing aid. A car radio, besides being a luxury, was an instrument for breaking day silence. He was a stickler for both day and night silence, although the former was not an absolutely total silence as was the latter.

St. Benedict says, "Monks should diligently cultivate silence at all times, but especially at night" (42:1) after the office of Compline. The silence after Compline, the night prayer, was called, in some monasteries, Grand Silence or

Greater Silence, the Lesser Silence being in the day. We were jarred into night silence with a loud blast from a battleship horn we'd procured from the Army-Navy surplus depot, not after Compline but after evening recreation, which ended at nine o'clock. Night silence ended after breakfast, at which time day silence began. In the old days, before Vatican II, the observance of night silence was rigidly enforced. But there were occasions when it was violated. Like the night some monks sneaked up to a room over the garage to listen to a championship boxing match on the radio. They were caught and made to kneel out in the refectory the next day at the noon meal. Now we may recreate beyond nine o'clock, but silence, for the benefit of monks who retire early, is protected on the floors where we have our private rooms.

When Brother Sebastian and I were novices, our classmates hijacked a monastery car on a starry December night and went to Milbank to look at the outdoor Christmas decorations. When it came time to give the signal for the beginning of night silence, neither Sebastian nor I volunteered to sound the horn for the novice whose duty it was that week, but who was out for a night on the town. Sebastian and I were miffed about having been left behind. In the morning, only two of the novices confessed their transgressions to the novice master for their absence without leave. But the rest were hauled in, and confessions were extracted from them. They all had to kneel in the refectory while Sebastian and I gloated.

Culpa was another discipline I had to learn. Private *culpa*, made to one's immediate superior, was for faults that couldn't be saved until the end of the week. At public *culpa* on Friday mornings everyone had to confess three faults. Of what things were we culpable? For breaking monastic property, for making noise in the corridor, for not rising promptly from sleep, for breaking night silence and day silence, for not keeping our hands under the scapular—to mention but a few. It was never difficult to come up with three faults for public *culpa*. Before there was an energy crunch, we apologized for leaving on lights. Before ecologists made everyone aware of the earth's shrinking water table, our cook apologized weekly for using too much water. What was so wrong about not keeping our hands under the scapular? We never asked, presuming this, too, was a custom of proper decorum.

The line in the corridor outside Father Meinrad's room was always long on Friday nights. That was the time for weekly confessions, when we got down to really serious business. We didn't confess our lapses in obeying rules like keeping our hands under our scapular. We told him our sins. Although Father Meinrad was a stern disciplinarian, he was also a compassionate and wise old man who understood human failings. It was obvious that he loved us regardless of our many infractions against discipline. In fact, it seemed that the monks he liked best were the ones who were always in trouble.

For ten years, I was the prior of this monastery. St. Benedict was wary of priors. He said, "Some priors, puffed up by the evil spirit of pride and thinking of themselves as second abbots, usurp tyrannical power and foster contention and discord in their communities" (65:2). I tried to avoid all of that.

I often wished that I could have been more like Father Prior Meinrad. Whenever I tried imitating his indubitable glare, my eyes crossed. Once I tacked a sign on the bulletin board informing the community that I'd been conscious of a lot of noise during the time for private spiritual reading—a radio being played, someone pushing a mop bucket down the hall, conversation in a room, the copy machine in use. A junior monk, who lived next to me, called my attention to another distraction during spiritual reading I had failed to list. The prior was clacking away at his typewriter, preparing his reprimand.

Titles and Names

I n recent years, Benedictine women have begun using the term "monastery" for their convents because they also live under the monastic Rule of St. Benedict. A monastery governed by an abbot or abbess is an abbey. There are only two abbeys of Benedictine women in this country.

When our motherhouse in Indiana celebrated its centenary in 1954, it was named an archabbey with an archabbot at its head. These are honorary titles. Neither the monastery nor its superior has any special privileges.

Nowadays all non-ordained monks are called "Brother." When I came to the monastery, a monk who was studying for the priesthood was called "Frater," the Latin word for brother, in order to distinguish him from the brother who was not destined for ordination. Priests were addressed as "Father." We were obliged to use the proper titles when speaking to one another. Nicknames were absolutely forbidden. If one resorted to that kind of name-calling, he had to confess it at *culpa*. Among our peers, we always felt free to speak to each other without using the proper title, but we were never so disrespectful as to address a senior monk by his name alone. This has changed over the years, but I'm sure not every older monk appreciates the informality. Nicknames are no longer a problem. Bestowing an unkind appellation on a monk is still a matter for *culpa*, however. We once heard someone confess, "For calling my confrere a big fat sow."

When we entered the monastery, everyone assumed a new name because he was beginning a new kind of life. Some monks—like Larry Hughes of the Bronx who became Cuthbert—must have surprised their parents with their choice of names. My mother suggested that I choose Dominic, but there was already a Brother Dominic in the community. These days we may keep the names we were given by our parents. When we were presented with this option, we were told that the names by which we were christened are now considered more important than the ones monks used to take upon entering the monastery. This notion stemmed from the teachings of Vatican Council II.

The story is told of a monk in another monastery who made it known that he was going to keep the name he had received in monastic life. "Why?" he was asked. "Are you afraid of losing your identity?" His was a community of over a hundred monks. His answer: "No, my laundry."

In former years, an abbot sometimes reserved the right to name his monks. Like a newborn child, the monk had no choice of what he was to be called. While I was visiting a monastery in England, one of the monks told me he'd had the name Ethelbert foisted on him. "I didn't know if I'd become a monk or a nun." He's now Charles, having resumed his baptismal name as soon as the opportunity arose.

It was the custom at Blue Cloud Abbey to receive your new name at first profession. When a novice was on retreat in preparation for making vows, he submitted a list of three names to the abbot. The abbot usually gave the novice his first choice if there didn't appear to be anything odd about the name.

All through the novitiate year, we researched Butler's *Lives of the Saints* in pursuit of a heavenly patron we liked but probably had no intention of emulating. We admitted to one another the names we were considering, but the professed members of the community weren't supposed to learn our names until we revealed them while reading our vow charts during the profession ceremony.

Somehow Brother Felix found out that I was going to be called Benedict. He protested to the abbot. There was a Frater Benedict in the community. Two Benedicts would complicate things for him in his position as monastery mailman. It didn't matter to Brother Felix that our last names were different or that one of us was Frater and the other Brother. My name was rescinded.

I hadn't wanted to be called Benedict anyway. My first choice was Benet, an Anglicized form of Benedict, also spelled Bennet and Bennett. I'd wanted St. Benet Biscop as my patron. Abbot Gilbert must have thought this was slighting our Holy Father Benedict. He wouldn't let me use either Benedict or Benet as long as I was associating it with Biscop. I was to have the Holy Patriarch of the Monks of the West as my saint. And this created the dilemma for Brother Felix.

On the eve before my profession day, I still didn't have a name. There had been no mention of giving me my second choice (Eric) or my third (Hugh). When we were standing in line for Compline, the novice master came up to me and whispered my new name. I was to be called Benet with St. Benedict of Nursia as my patron, not the English bibliophile and collector of art—the kind of saint I admired and would have eagerly emulated. Years later when I took over the management of our bookstore, I called it The St. Benet Biscop Shop. Some customers think it's named for me.

Now that we may keep the names given to us at baptism, some monks share the same name. We've had more than one Lawrence, Peter, Michael, Christopher, and Thomas.

It is unlikely that future novices, even if they wish to change their names, will choose the names of Benedictine saints. We'll have no more monks named Odo, Odilo, Placid, Maur, Wilfrid, Bede. And no more Cuthberts. Probably no more Benets. Father Odo and Father Odilo often felt it necessary to explain to people that their uncommon names had come from two saintly abbots of Cluny, the great medieval French abbey. The former used to spell his name when meeting strangers. "Father Odo—O-d-o." One time he introduced himself to a woman in this manner. She in turn introduced him to someone else as "Father Odo Odio."

Father Odilo is careful about enouncing his name when meeting strangers. "O-d-low," he says. A visitor once thought he'd introduced himself as O. D. Lowe.

The Holy Habit

The image of a Franciscan friar is often used for marketing purposes. I've even seen him on labels and in advertising for goods produced by Benedictines. The friar, in his brown robe girded by a rope with a big wooden rosary dangling from it, is more appealing than the monk in his drab black habit that lacks any accessories. Most Benedictines wear black. One congregation wears a dark blue habit; two others wear white. Two monasteries in this country have chosen to wear a gray tunic and black scapular, an apron-like covering of equal length in front and back, worn over the tunic. Monks of another community wear a short habit made of denim.

There is also a variation in habit style. Some hoods are detachable. The Austrian Congregation, however, doesn't even wear a hood. The English Congregation has two wide lapels on its hood that hang over the front of the scapular. I've heard them called "tit warmers." The Swiss have a long hood, reaching to the middle of the back, that I've heard referred to as a "potato sack" or a "jockstrap."

The habit we wear is composed of a black tunic and scapular with a hood sewn to it. A black leather belt is worn around the tunic, and the scapular hangs freely in front and back.

The habit is received upon entrance to the novitiate, the initial year of monastic formation. At the profession of final vows, the monk is clothed in a *cuculla*, an ample black robe with wide sleeves, which we used to wear to Mass and Vespers. Never in the summer, though. Now the only time a monk of our community wears the *cuculla* is during the rite of final profession.

Since the 1970s, the habit has become a garment donned mostly for the Divine Office and Mass. We no longer have to wear it to every meal (supper only) or at recreation. It was never worn when we were engaged in manual work or athletic activities, though our founding members recall the humid summer days back in Indiana when they had to play softball in their habits. They also remember being required to put on swimming trunks under their habits before disrobing. We were never that modest here.

If anyone in Marvin was ever doubtful that monks had actually settled in the neighborhood, they were quickly able to identify us by our attire. We wore our habits to the Marvin Hall, where we went to vote and sometimes to entertain at neighborhood gatherings. I once went into the Marvin Bar in my habit and no one batted an eye.

We dressed rather uniformly when I entered the monastery, even when we weren't wearing monastic habits. Clothing and shoes were purchased for us by the lot. There was only one kind of work shoe and one style of black oxfords. The manual laborers wore blue jeans and overalls, and those monks with more domestic jobs wore gray cotton twills. Shirts of different colors, but all of the same cut, were available. It really didn't matter how we dressed in the house, but when we went away from the monastery on business trips or to attend public functions, a black suit and clerical or brother's collar (with a notch in it to distinguish him from a priest) was the only proper attire. I've never been a clothes hound, so I've never paid much attention to what we wore. But I thought it was gauche for a monk to wear white socks with a black suit, as some of them did.

St. Benedict said monks should "sleep clothed, and girded with belts or cords; but they should remove their knives, lest they accidentally cut themselves in their sleep. Thus the monks will always be ready to arise without delay when the signal is given; each will hasten to arrive at the Work of God before the others, yet with all dignity and decorum" (22:5-6).

We've never slept in our habits. But in order to pay homage to this instruction of St. Benedict's, the monks used to wear night scapulars to bed. The night scapular covered the shoulders and had no hood attached to it. Father Gerald wore his night scapular around an ankle because he was fearful of being strangled in his sleep. Nowadays, if you mention the night scapular to one of the younger monks, he doesn't know what you're talking about.

I've forgotten all the prayers we were supposed to say while putting on the habit—a prayer for each article. I do remember the belt's prayer referring to "the girdle of righteousness." Both the night scapular and the dressing prayers fell by the wayside with the modernization of monasticism by Vatican II.

Profession

"Uphold me, O Lord, and I shall live. And do not let me be confounded in my expectations." These are the words a monk sings three times in the ceremony of his solemn profession of vows. But only an extremely naive person would enter a monastery and expect to be free of all troubles, to never be confounded.

St. Benedict says that anyone who becomes an abbot must learn to adapt himself to a variety of characters. Each of us brings his own individuality to the monastery and keeps it. If some of us have unpleasant characteristics, we are encouraged to change them. The monk is told he must become a new man, but no one ever succeeds in totally wiping out the old man who accompanies him into the monastery. Of the monks he must govern, St. Benedict tells the abbot that he must know "what a difficult and demanding burden he has undertaken: directing souls and serving a variety of temperaments, coaxing, reproving and encouraging them as appropriate" (2:31).

While we are encouraged to modify some of our habits, conformity is required in many other areas. It is believed that a monastery will function tranquilly if everyone will do the same things at the same time. But every monastery has a quota of nonconformists. Sometimes they are even held in high esteem.

Even before he makes his final vows, a monk knows pretty well what to expect of himself. His temperament and his abilities determine how he carries out the assignments given to him in monastic life. He knows what he can accomplish and he knows his limitations. Monastic life teaches us to have the humility to accept who we are and what we can do. St. Benedict does not subject a monk to blind obedience in the performance of a task that will discourage him: "Should he see, however, that the weight of the burden is altogether too much for his strength, then he should choose the appropriate moment and explain patiently to his superior the reasons why he cannot perform the task" (68:2).

Like anyone, a monk usually becomes confounded when he tries to do something he can't or to be someone he isn't. Now and then a monk in mufti will try concealing his true identity in the presence of strangers, usually to spare himself from being questioned to death by the curious. A confrere of mine, when asked by a man on a train what his occupation was, replied that he sold insurance. The fellow traveler began asking him questions about insurance policies. That put an end to the bluffing. "Speak the truth with heart and tongue" (4:27), St. Benedict admonishes in the chapter on "The Tools of Good Works."

The monk has a vow of poverty, but what monk has to live in a state of poverty? Nowadays we shy away from using that term. We speak of "common ownership" or "sharing of goods." St. Benedict clearly wants a monastic community to live in a relative state of comfort. A monastery should be constructed with all necessities in it, he says. As for the individual monk, some of us have greater personal needs than others. "Whoever needs less should thank God and not be distressed," St. Benedict says, "but whoever needs more should feel humble because of his weakness, not self-important because of the kindness shown him" (34:3-4).

We have changed our procedure with regard to procuring items for personal use. When I came to the monastery, a monk had to draw up a shopping list that was initialed by his superior. This list was given to the monk in charge of the vestry. "I, Brother Benet, humbly request: 1 tube of toothpaste and 1 pair of pajamas." Nowadays, we have a closet in which toiletries may be obtained without anyone's permission. In former times, after-shave lotion was frowned upon and scented soap forbidden. When I was allowed to let my hair grow after novitiate, I was not permitted to shampoo it, and I could not use deodorant when I was a sweating young monk. Such grooming practices were considered unmonastic. Now I have to make a choice of which shampoo and which deodorant to use.

Now we are allowed to carry a sensible amount of money in our billfolds. I can remember going to a movie, a rare treat in the old days, and having the good luck of being given a quarter to spend for popcorn. In those days, you felt very worldly having a quarter in your pocket. Now we can go out to a movie whenever we wish and have enough money to buy the largest bucket of buttered popcorn.

"St. Benedict is turning over in his grave," our assistant treasurer said to me while sorting through a stack of canceled checks. I could have quoted the Rule with regard to some monks having greater needs than others. But I didn't, because one or more of those checks might have been used to purchase items for me that the assistant treasurer would have thought superfluous.

When I came to the monastery, I knew that a candidate for this kind of life had to dispose of his personal property. I didn't own much, just a lot of books, and I gave away most of them.

The few I brought with me were confiscated upon my arrival. These were novels, some of which I'd read in a contemporary literature class at college. My novels were locked up in the devil's closet, a place where forbidden books were kept in a large padlocked wire cage. These books were no longer my possessions, and neither would they become the community's property. They belonged to the devil. I couldn't understand why books that were required reading in one Benedictine community were banned in another. Today my bookcase holds a lot more books than I brought with me to the monastery in 1958. The assistant treasurer may have come across a check used in payment for purchases of mine from the book club to which I belong.

Monks don't need the best, the newest, the state-of-the-art. But though there are sufficient warnings against materialism in St. Benedict's Rule, the truth of the matter is that we give in to these temptations. This is also the truth: No matter how much monks give away, no matter how frugally we live, monks will never be poor.

One of the ironies of monasticism is that when a monk professes his solemn vows, he makes out a last will and testament in which he gives away everything that he may still own, and he renounces his right to inherit anything. After he has dispossessed himself, the monk settles down to a life in which he is assured that whatever is needed will be provided.

If we now have a more liberal interpretation of poverty, so have we a different understanding of celibacy. When I was in the novitiate, the novice master spoke to us about sex only once, but that was for a whole class period. He told us how to behave in the presence of women, and he told us how to behave among ourselves. "If I ever see two novices going down the corridor holding hands, I shall have to correct them." (That could be another reason we were advised to keep our hands under the scapular!) In those days, there was more concern about a particular friendship between two monks than there was about a friendship between a monk and a woman. It was difficult for a novice to become intimate with a woman since there weren't many around in those days, but the possibility of becoming too intimate with a fellow novice was always present. There was an underlying fear that if you had a particular friend in the community, one thing could lead to another. The fear of intimacy was so great that when one monk went to another monk's room, the door had to be kept open.

In reality, everyone had a personal friend and still has. It is the most ordinary thing in the world to confide in a special friend of one's own sex. Another reality is that a monk, regardless of his sexual orientation, is required to be celibate. St. Aelred, abbot of Rievaulx, encouraged friendships among his medieval monks in England. His treatise *On Spiritual Friendship* has contributed greatly to dispelling all scorn for particular friendships. He is the saint who offers the monk of our time a model for the kind of intimate relationship he may legitimately and lovingly form. These are sentiments addressed to Ivo, his monk-friend: "Here we are, you and I, and I hope a third, Christ, is in our midst. There is no one now to disturb us; there is no one to break in upon our friendly chat, no man's prattle or noise of any kind will creep into this pleasant solitude. Come now, beloved, open your heart, and pour into the ears of a friend whatever you will, and let us accept gracefully this place, time, and leisure." Given the climate in seminaries and religious houses these days, I hope there will be no ban placed on reading Aelred, as was the case with an older generation of monks.

Be careful of forming an inseparable relationship with another monk. Practice custody of the eyes and ears. These were the admonitions we also received in our monastic formation. In the days when we were begging money for building the monastery, the whole community assembled four times a year to prepare direct mailings. The stuffing of envelopes with appeal letters was considered tedious work. The rule of day silence prevented us from breaking the monotony with conversation, but we were allowed to listen to music. Someone put on a recording of the Broadway musical *The King and I*. When Father Prior Meinrad heard "We Kiss in a Shadow" being sung, he promptly ordered the record removed from the turntable.

"Why," I once asked, "don't we ever get the magazine section of the Sunday paper?" It was explained to me that women's lingerie advertisements appeared there. We might be tempted to ogle over women in their undergarments. It was this same sense of precaution that led to inking out, in the pages of *National Geographic*, the breasts of women who lived in places with a tropical climate.

If a monk is more comfortable materially and less paranoid about his sexuality, where does he stand on the matter of vowed obedience? St. Benedict appears willing to let a monk negotiate with the abbot when obedience seems difficult or impossible. "If after the explanation the superior is still determined to hold to his original order, then the junior must recognize that this is best for him. Trusting in God's help, he must in love obey" (68:4-5). These are the words of a reasonable man.

Some people are asked to obey in opposition to what conscience and experience tell them is right, but in the monastery most of our obedience is rendered without inner conflict. Obedience may be irksome at times, but it's seldom impossible.

Even Love One Another

Followers of St. Benedict should be found "earnestly competing in obedience to one another" (72:6). Not only that, St. Benedict says we should respect and love each other. All of this is easier said than done, but it must be done. This is our Christian calling.

We certainly learn to live with our differences in a monastic community. I may find myself praying in choir alongside someone with whom I am at odds in practically everything, but I cannot go to another choir stall, I am assigned to sit next to him, my brother in the monastery. This is exactly what we need to do: We need to pray together, to pray side by side in order to bring about a healing, to no longer be alienated. When we clasp the other's hand at the greeting of peace, we should really mean what we say: "Peace be with you."

St. Benedict tells his monks, "Your way of acting should be different from the world's way; the love of Christ must come before all else. You are not to act in anger or nurse a grudge. Rid your heart of all deceit. Never give a hollow greeting of peace or turn away when someone needs your love" (4:20–26).

I'm thinking of Matthew. He came to us in his late teens, having dropped out of college to enter our novitiate. He was a handsome young man, a descendant of the Dark Irish. He smiled a lot and could laugh off some of the inane things we took seriously. Some monks thought Matthew was naive; others said he was guileless. We all agreed that Matthew was helpful and often asked him to do our housework or other chores. He always replied with a ready, "Sure." "Matthew, could I get you to take my place on dishes after lunch and probably after supper too?"

"Sure."

"Matthew, would you clean the recreation room while I'm away?"

"Sure."

Often he would ask, "Need any help?"

I should have known that he didn't have a monastic vocation: I never heard him complain about anything in the several months he was here.

Matthew went back to college. He visited us only a few times in the following years. We lost touch with him, although we'd heard that he'd gone to graduate school in New York and had decided to stay out there.

And then the phone call came from his mother. Matthew was dying at the age of thirty. He felt that the church had rejected him for being gay and for having AIDS. He wanted to die without the benefits of the church. Never "turn away when someone needs your love." Two of our monks went to Matthew's bedside. He recognized them as friends who loved him.

St. Benedict teaches us that a community can live in mutual respect and love regardless of the differences among its members. Of course there are flare-ups within a community. Our anger is not always controlled. Once when several of us were watching Glenda Jackson's portrayal of Elizabeth I on *Masterpiece Theatre*, a monk walked into the TV room and stationed himself in front of the set, blocking our view, and announced, "This is not the set for PBS."

"Sit down," one of the viewers said. "We can't see the screen."

"You're not supposed to be watching PBS in here. The TV next door is reserved for PBS."

"If you don't get out of here," another viewer threatened, "I'll knock you on your ass."

"Do you think you can do it?" asked the legalist.

"No, but I'll get help."

I'm sure the rest of us would have come to his assistance.

Even senior monks can lose their cool. At coffee break, one of the elders was angry with the abbot and prior who had been teasing him about something. He poured his coffee over their heads. "If you have a dispute with someone," St. Benedict says, "make peace with him before the sun goes down" (4:73). The elder begged an apology on the spot. I once said some unkind words to a confrere, and apologized immediately. Two weeks later, he came to my room and told me that he had forgiven me. I thanked him.

"But don't you ever let it happen again," he said.

The first reality a person faces upon entering a monastic community is an awareness that these are not the people with whom one would choose to live under normal circumstances. But St. Benedict tells us that regardless of the monks' differences, God loves us all equally and we must love one another.

Some people are not accepted into the community because it is obvious at the moment of inquiry that they will never fit in. Others leave our community because they no longer fit in. Nevertheless, we have ended up with a lot of diverse kinds of people attempting to live together compatibly. Sometimes we fail.

A fellow monk told me about having unearthed a list of community members on which the notable characteristic of each monk was succinctly identified by two words after the name. For example: Father Benno—"humility personified." Since my name was not on the list, I suggested it might make interesting table reading. But my informant said that some of the monks who are still alive would not appreciate these brief descriptions of themselves. I presume that not all of the labels are as complimentary as Father Benno's.

Reading St. Benedict's Rule easily dispels the idealized notion of all monks being holy. These are the words he uses to describe some of the people who live in monasteries: undisciplined, restless, negligent, rebellious, arrogant, luke-warm, and slothful. And the list goes on. No doubt some of these same words are used in the list that describes monks who live or once lived in this monastery.

"Do not aspire to be called holy before you really are, but first be holy that you may more truly be called so" (4:62). St. Benedict is reasonably sure that his disciples will make strides in the direction of holiness, and he reminds us that we are always in a state of conversion. Conversion is another vow made by Benedictines. St. Benedict sees it as an ongoing process, a striving to make things better. Our spiritual life is expected to improve, and so is the performance of our natural abilities. Take pride in your work; improve it.

Aim for perfection, St. Benedict says. And be patient. St. Benedict is the patron of patience. We see how willing he is to give people more than one chance. He tells us to be patient with ourselves. In the Rule, he shows us where to start in our advance toward holiness, but his guidebook is not a manual for instant self-improvement. He sets no deadlines. We have a whole lifetime in which to amend our faults by persevering in the monastery.

The Abbot

St. Benedict said an abbot should "strive to be loved rather than feared" (64:15). Somewhere along the way, the monks began fearing even the abbots who were loved. Abbot Gilbert came to office at a time when customs differed from our present manner of relating to an abbot. Besides the ritual of kissing his ring, we had to rise to our feet whenever the abbot approached a group of seated monks. Whenever he left the group, we again had to stand to attention. Even the sole monk relaxing in a comfortable chair with the evening paper had to stand if the abbot walked into the community room. I always thought this was rather pretentious. Abbot Gilbert was such an ordinary person. Nevertheless, we all adhered to established decorum in the presence of the abbot. This was not the case with Abbot Gilbert's immediate successor. When a monk accused him of cheating in a handball game, a heated argument was pursued on the court.

I was always submissive and timid whenever Abbot Gilbert summoned me to his office. Once my delicate conscience led me to his office. During my vacation, instead of going directly to my parental home in Casselton, North Dakota, I had accompanied my parents on a trip to Ontario, Canada, and

New York City. When I confessed this to Abbot Gilbert, I was expecting a reproof for not having sought his permission for such an extended trip. He only said, "That's all right, Brother. Just don't tell anyone."

Abbot Gilbert received me into the novitiate and heard my profession of first and final vows. On the day of my simple profession, he told my mother that this act had restored me to my baptismal innocence. "If your son died today, he'd go straight to heaven." She replied, "I hope he doesn't."

After his resignation from the abbacy, Abbot Gilbert worked away from the monastery as a chaplain and then a pastor. One time he thought he was being given the runaround with regard to procuring a car. I was prior of the monastery by then, and he complained to me because the abbot was not at home. He said, "That place is even more bureaucratic than when I was running it." I told him to go out and buy a car. "Don't get a Cadillac, though, or they'll be all over my back." He bought a used Mercury and drove it until he retired and returned to the monastery.

In his later years, those of us who had entered the monastery when he was abbot found it easier to relate to him. He'd become more like us. And more like his true self. One day he and I were talking about the old pontifical ceremonial and all the vesture in which an abbot was clad. He said, "I can't imagine wearing all that junk nowadays." Perhaps he was referring especially to the two silk dalmatics, which some of the monks irreverently called "liturgical lingerie," and the buskins, which other monks called "liturgical booties." The dalmatic, like a woman's slip, was worn underneath the chasuble, the outer liturgical vestment. I never bothered asking our liturgist why the abbot had to wear two of them. The buskins were ceremonial stockings matching the color of the chasuble.

During Abbot Gilbert's administration, our community doubled in membership. No doubt he was saddened, as we all were, when monks began departing in those years after Vatican II, but he bore no resentment. When former members and their families were invited to the monastery for a reunion several years later, Abbot Gilbert preached at Mass on the last day of the gathering. He began by saying, "When I look out here and see so many children, I tell myself that I must be the grandpa."

He had attended three sessions of the Vatican Council, representing the monastic federation to which our community belongs. The era of the sixties was a difficult time for all abbots. Some monks were eager for change, and others resented it. Although Abbot Gilbert was a Latin scholar, he offered no resistance to the introduction of the vernacular into our liturgy. In his first letter to us from Rome, he reported that at the opening session of the Council the participants took an oath to uphold the faith but no mention was made of upholding secrecy. "One of the abbots remarked to me that the only secret that is to be kept is that we are getting nothing done." When Abbot Gilbert returned from that first session, he talked to the community about the Council one evening and responded to our questions. I asked if he'd verify what I'd read in *Time* about American Cardinals Spellman and Cushing feuding over the proposal to use native languages in the liturgy. "I'm absolutely forbidden to make any comment," he replied.

Vatican II intended to modernize the Catholic Church and even the ancient institution of monasticism. We suddenly found ourselves with new freedoms and practices. We no longer had to be in bed at an early hour. We were able to talk at breakfast and at the noon meal. Women were invited into the refectory.

Even prior to the Vatican Council, our monastery had a reputation for making changes and adaptations. Before we received our independence from the mother abbey, Abbot Ignatius, on one of his visits from Indiana, observed, "Blue Cloud is the most independent dependent foundation St. Meinrad's has ever made." We saw no need to follow St. Meinrad's schedule. Morning rising was later here than at the motherhouse and so was the hour for retiring. A longer recreation period was allowed because of the hard physical work involved in the construction of our own monastery.

In 1960, Abbot Gilbert bought us a television set. Perhaps ours was the first monastery in the country to have a TV inside the cloister. Monks who belonged to houses that ran schools had to sneak over to a student dormitory in order to watch television, but our set was abbatially approved. Although our viewing was restricted in the beginning to only certain nights and particular programs, we were happy for this privilege. On a Saturday in February, however, soon after the purchase of the TV, a good number of monks were caught watching a play about Abraham Lincoln during night silence. "Turn off that TV!" Abbot Gilbert shouted. "And don't turn it on for a week." While viewing John F. Kennedy's inauguration, I was making comments to a confrere and was told to be quiet. "You're breaking day silence," Abbot Gilbert reminded me. There were also occasions when he called me to his office after having received reports of my breaking night silence.

As long as there are monks alive who knew him, some of Abbot Gilbert's mannerisms will be imitated whenever we recall our first abbot—his habit of speaking out of the side of his mouth and grabbing your elbow when he had something to relate. And the occasional *non sequitur* that monks found even more baffling because a professor of logic had spoken it.

 *A Public Place*

"This place is a public monastery," Brother Patrick used to say whenever the number of guests in the house exceeded that of the monks. There is an unending fascination with monasteries. A young woman from England told me, "Yours is the first monastery I've visited which hasn't been in ruins."

"Is this a Catholic church?" I was asked while conducting a tour of the monastery one Sunday afternoon. "Where are the statues?" the woman asked.

"We have only one statue in our church," I informed her.

"Where is the statue? I don't see it."

"Over here." I led her to the Lady Chapel. "Our Lady has her own little church."

The woman wailed, "Oh, Mary, they have shoved you off to a corner."

I suggested that we continue looking at the rest of the church. In the sanctuary, she went to the altar and grabbed the cloth covering it. "Look at this!" she exclaimed to her male companion. "A horse blanket! They've put a horse blanket on the altar." The man said nothing, but I could tell he agreed with her.

The altar cloth, woven in shades of gold and brown, was the work of Brother Micah. He had spent weeks at the loom and was pleased with his accomplishment.

"The weaver would not appreciate your comment," I responded calmly.

Another tourist found displeasure with the stained-glass windows. "They're too modern," she complained.

Again, calmly, I tried defending our house of prayer. "This church happens to have been built in the present century."

Of course not everyone finds fault with the building. Some people have found peace in it. A man told me of how healing had come to him while praying there in the predawn solitude. A great burden had been lifted from him. Another man was able to recognize that his grieving for a deceased parent had been inadequate, and he was able to finish it one night while here on retreat.

St. Benedict said no monastery would ever be without guests. Certainly ours is never without them. It became a Benedictine tradition to offer not only spiritual but also bodily sustenance to all callers at the monastery. A medieval monastic customary describes the duties of the guest master. These include providing guests with bedding that is kept "sweet and clean" and "two hogsheads of wine." St. Benedict says nothing in his Rule about the duration of a guest's stay. In a sixteenth-century English monastery, a number of guests—a husband and wife and their seven children—extended their stay to seven years. No doubt St. Benedict would have considered this immoderate.

Sometimes monks themselves are guests of other monasteries, and St. Benedict tells them how to behave. A visiting monk should "be content with the life as he finds it" in another monastery. But, "he may, indeed, with all humility and love make some reasonable criticism or observations, which the abbot should prudently consider; it is possible that the Lord guided him to the monastery for this very purpose" (61:2–4).

One time, Father Ray brought home two young men who were hitchhiking on Highway 12. They were wearing white bed sheets and were barefooted. The sheets needed washing and so did the individuals wrapped in them. In St. Benedict's day, the abbot washed the feet of guests, but we showed these particular guests to the showers and offered to wash their sheets. One of the sheets was badly ripped in the washing machine, and we had to replace it with one of our own. The young men were itinerant preachers of the gospel, and as such wore nothing beneath their robes fashioned from bed sheets. On the windy day of their intended departure, they feared being exposed. The two disciples spent another day with us.

"We preach pure religion," one of them told me. "We own no church buildings or trappings of any kind."

"People who put statues in churches are idolaters," the other said.

I was relieved we have only one statue in our church.

Some monastery guests do present problems. We had one who upset our carpenter by using monastery lumber for making boomerangs. Lots of boomerangs, some of which the guest himself put in the gift shop to sell.

Not all guests appreciate us. There was a fellow from California who shut himself into a guest room for several days, studying Scripture. His conclusion was expressed in a note we found on the desk: "In the Book of Revelation, the dragon with seven heads is the Catholic Church."

Monks know that someone will always come looking for them and find them at home. It is of great importance for us to provide peace to everyone who comes into our monastic home, and even when we monks think we're in a state of upheaval or living under a certain amount of tension, guests will tell us of the peace they've found here. Once a departing guest told me, "It's been so peaceful at the abbey."

"Good heavens!" I exclaimed. "Don't you know the abbot has just resigned?"

St. Benedict said guests should be "welcomed as Christ." A nun, who was conducting a retreat at our monastery for women who had been hurt by men, called three of the monks aside and told them how grateful she was to the monastic community for being kind to these retreatants. "Gentle," she said. "Unlike those other men." We were amazed because it had not been apparent to us that anyone had been making a conscious effort. Although St. Benedict admonishes us to welcome all guests as Christ, we are sometimes surprised to learn that we have been doing just that.

 *The Pilgrim*

Monastic communities throughout the country knew Patrick Sean O'Mahoney, but none of us knew very much about him. He told conflicting stories. The first time he showed up here, Pat informed us he'd been a monk in Scotland during his youth. On another visit, he said he was still a member of an English monastery. "I've been away too long. It's time I think of going back."

He died on the street in San Diego. The police found a phone number on his person for a nearby Benedictine monastery. Monks from there were able to identify the corpse.

A monk of another monastery told me that Pat had been thinking of "retiring" because age was catching up with him. He was in his eighties and had spent much of his adult life wandering from monastery to monastery. He'd been coming to ours for thirty years. A nursing brotherhood in Canada had offered to look after him whenever he decided to leave the road.

I once found him right in the middle of the road—U.S. Highway 12. Someone called from the bus depot in Milbank and informed me that an elderly man was being left off below the Marvin hill and he wished to be met by a monk. I sensed this could be no one other than Patrick Sean O'Mahoney. When I found him, he was standing in the middle of the highway, praying the rosary, wearing a wide-brim straw hat, a clerical shirt, and a pectoral cross. He begged his clothing from monks, and this particular hat looked Cistercian, the kind those monks used to wear when working in the fields; the shirt could have come from any monk, Benedictine or Cistercian. But how had he obtained a pectoral cross? Had he actually talked some abbot out of his cross?

He usually stayed with us two or three days; then we bought him a bus ticket and sent him on his way to the next monastery. He once spent an entire winter at a monastery because he'd fallen and broken a leg. Although it's really very doubtful that Pat was a monk, St. Benedict identified monks whose behavior was no different from Pat's. St. Benedict called them "gyrovagues who spend their entire lives drifting from region to region, staying as guests for three or four days in different monasteries. Always on the move, they never settle down, and are slaves to their own wills and gross appetites" (2:10-11).

Pat presented us with a list of foods he liked, and he appreciated being waited on in our refectory. The guest master never failed in charity. He washed Pat's clothing and replaced items that had worn out.

Pat was a portly man. It was obvious that monasteries had kept him nourished. Although he was bald on top, monastery barbers were asked to trim what hair he had. One time he fussed because our barber wouldn't attend to him on demand. Pat came to my office complaining. He picked up a pair of scissors and began trimming his hair, which fell all over my desk.

When he joined us at the Divine Office, some monks were upset by his unwillingness to pray in unison. Now and then he departed from our text and prayed spontaneously. Because he'd been to so many monasteries, he considered himself an authority on monastic observance. He unhesitatingly corrected us for what he thought were improprieties in our household.

Once when one of our monks arrived at a monastery in another part of the country, the porter was fuming. "That goddamn Patrick Sean O'Mahoney is back with us," he said. The porter must have been having an overall bad day. Of a porter, St. Benedict says, "As soon as anyone knocks, or a poor man calls out, he replies, 'Thanks be to God' or 'Your blessing, please'" (66:3-4).

Are You Real People? 🌷

E very year students who are enrolled in sociology and
anthropology classes at a community college come
here on a field trip to study people like us. They also visit
a Hutterite colony and an Indian reservation. Benedictines,
Hutterites, and Native Americans are subjects of interest
because we all live apart from mainstream society. We belong
to "intentional communities." On a particular day, however,
members of each group may be found shopping at Wal-Mart.
After all, we are not totally withdrawn from the world.

Sometimes I've helped guide the college students through
the monastery and answered their questions. "What draws
men to a place like this?" "What are the drawbacks?" "What
do you do for recreation?" "Do you ever play pranks on each
other?" Fortunately, they have to leave before the questions
become too personal. Once one of them asked the abbot,
"Was your father also an abbot?"

On another occasion after the students had watched our
video about monastic life, a student inquired of Father Thomas,
"Do you think you guys will ever get married?" They had just
come from the Hutterite community where marriage had contributed to the propagation of that intentional community.

When I was the community's vocation director, I was now and then invited to speak at high-school religion classes. "Do you ever get bored?" "Do you have your own car?" "Are you ever given any money?" I always came away from these sessions convinced that most young people are not particularly interested in monasticism. Stability, for one thing, is a hard concept for them to grasp. This is understandable. It is so much easier to get about in the world nowadays, and there are so many different career choices for the young.

Although I have been to Europe twice and have lived in Ireland for the good part of a summer, I was close to thirty before I traveled beyond the Dakotas and Minnesota for the first time, and that was all the way to Missouri. When I entered the monastery, I presumed that I'd never go anywhere. The students thought it was simply incredible when I told them I had lived in the same place for almost forty years. My way of life seemed so restrictive to them. I had given up my freedom. I had become a slave of routine. There were usually moans from the audience when I explained that monks get up at the same time every day and do the same things day after day.

"Are you always able to procure the things you want?" a college student asked me. No. Only a month before the students' field trip to the monastery, I had been on vacation and had gone to an exhibit of photographs at a gallery. There were a couple of photographs I admired very much, and I asked if prints were available. "You may buy this book in which all of the photographs appear," the gallery clerk told me. I explained that I had to buy a bus ticket and didn't have any extra cash. "You may write a check." She was surprised when I admitted that I had no checking account. No plastic. But even though I may not be able to procure everything I want, I have everything I need.

Can You Laugh? 🌱

St. Francis of Assisi claimed the Lord had called upon him to be "a fool and simpleton." Our Holy Father Benedict certainly does not leave us with a similar impression of himself. Nor does he appear to tolerate silly behavior among his followers. One of the steps of humility in his Rule is "that [a monk] not be given to ready laughter . . ." (7:59). This conforms to another of St. Benedict's steps of humility. "A monk speaks gently and without laughter, seriously and with becoming modesty, briefly and reasonably, but without raising his voice . . ." (7:60).

Abbot Maurus Wolter, the nineteenth-century founder of Beuron Abbey in Germany, described the demeanor of a monk this way: "Let your carriage be manly and erect, in keeping with monastic discipline, but with the head bowed down slightly forward, not nervously moving from left to right, not sanctimoniously hanging to one side. The countenance should bear evidence of a holy and cheerful dignity, as the expression of a heart that is truly joyous. Care must be taken, however, not to burst forth in uncontrolled or frivolous laughter, not to take part in buffoonery."

It appears that buffoons are simply not tolerated in the Order of St. Benedict. The novice master told us St. Benedict opposed laughter, which led to buffoonery. But I wondered, as I read more about Abbot Maurus, if he found any kind of laughter suitable. Most monks of older generations were trained in proper bearing, and when I entered the monastery the influence of people like Maurus Wolter was evident in how we were instructed to conduct ourselves. Besides being instructed to keep our hands under the scapular, we were told not to cross our legs. "Control your eyes." "Sit up straight." "No singing in the shower."

The truth of the matter is that most monks laugh. They laugh a whole lot. How could we have endured all of these many centuries without joyfulness that is expressed in laughter? I suspect we have even produced more than one buffoon.

Our community has produced a clown in costume and makeup. Father Bernardine is a speaking clown, not a mime. He took up the practice because he wanted to amuse and inspire hospitalized children.

Father Bernardine doesn't have to put on a clown's attire in order to entertain, however. He has a joke or humorous story for every occasion. One particular routine of his involves barking in the ear of the listener. He has barked in the ears of bishops and abbots. He has no inhibitions. Not even when it comes to telling the story that ends with his planting a kiss on the listener's cheek. Father Bernardine was my novitiate classmate. One day the novice master gave us copies of the *Tyrocinium*, a manual of piety used by novices in American Benedictine monasteries in the years before Vatican II. When Father Bernardine came to the section on sensuality and its prohibition of a monk's smelling flowers and petting dogs, he declared, "This is a lot of medieval bullshit." We were all grateful to him. The novice master collected the books and we never had to use them.

 Books

A Benedictine monastery would be incomplete without a library. Over the ages, monks have valued their books, and still do today. Once when the Abbey of Monte Cassino was on the verge of being sacked, the monks fled with their library books and left behind the remains of St. Benedict. St. Francis chided one of his followers for wanting to own a Psalter. If the friar were given one book, Francis feared he would become a collector and would eventually own a library. Then, God forbid, he would be no different from a Benedictine.

We not only read books, we have them read to us. "Reading will always accompany the meals of the brothers," St. Benedict stipulates in his Rule. We hear fewer books these days because reading accompanies only the evening meal.

When I came to the monastery, the autobiography of Joe E. Brown, a comedian with an enormous mouth, was being read. Shortly before this, *The Doctors Mayo* was the table reading, but it had to be discontinued. The descriptions of surgeries and diseases were deemed unsuitable for mealtime listening.

There is always disagreement among the monks regarding the selections for table reading. I think *Jonathan Livingston*

Seagull was the most controversial book ever read in our refectory. Some monks praised it, and others panned it. I can't remember why. Was it because some monks admired Jonathan who soared like a free spirit, while others considered him a selfish bird that was only out to do his own thing? Although it is a slim book and could have been read in its entirety within the course of several meals, we had to put it aside in order to restore peace in the refectory.

What inspires some monks bores others. Or irritates them. I can think of one book that everybody disliked: *The Collected Poems of Father Leonard Feeney*. Although some of the monks had undoubtedly memorized poems by Father Feeney in their Catholic childhoods, his work seemed like doggerel now. Loud groans were heard throughout the meals. Finally, one of the monks hid the book from the reader.

For a while, the table reader was allowed to choose his own material. Now one person is in charge of selecting the books. He has two consultants, who agree with him most of the time.

The language used in books offends some monks. After one reader repeated the slang word for defecation several times, all table readers were notified never to read that word aloud. The next evening, the same reader introduced two more words that are now forbidden forever in table reading. One of these words appears in Kathleen Norris's *The Cloister Walk*. I was a guest at a monastery where the book was being read soon after its publication. The table reader said the word. At Blue Cloud, we found a substitute for it when the book was read in our refectory.

Listening to the reading of *The Cloister Walk* caused Abbot Thomas to comment, "Kathleen has a greater appreciation for monasticism than some monks have." Monastic men and women agree that she has a keen perception of what we're all about. I recall my great satisfaction in hearing her quoted in a conference during our community retreat, conducted by a monk of another abbey. This was after she'd first begun writing about people who live in cloisters. Now, she is asked by monastics themselves to be their retreat master.

Prayer

"That we will all learn to respect the various types of spirituality people have and that we will always refrain from ridiculing a piety that differs from ours." Abbot Thomas prayed this at Mass one day during the intercessions. I find myself guilty of Benedictine chauvinism from time to time. Sometimes I'm irritated by the religious practices of other people, especially when they tell me, "This is what you should be doing in the monastery." I make snide remarks, despite my deep belief that other forms of piety are legitimate and must be respected. Perhaps the abbot had me in mind with his petition.

There is a distinct form of Benedictine spirituality to which everyone conforms in order to be Benedictine, and it is this that draws people to monastic life. Nevertheless, other types of prayer and devotions may be part of one's spiritual life as well. A Benedictine has every right to complain if vespers should ever be replaced by the recitation of the rosary or a charismatic prayer meeting. This does not mean that Benedictines never pray the rosary or take part in charismatic prayer. It simply means that these two forms of prayer are not the kind to which we are called by profession. The prayer to which nothing else is to be preferred by us is the Divine Office. It is our tradition.

The hours of the Divine Office are made up of hymns, psalms, antiphons, readings, intercessions, and responsories. Before Vatican II, there were eight offices: matins, the longest (also called vigils or the office of readings), prayed after midnight or anticipated the evening before; lauds at the crack of dawn; prime, the first office prayed in daylight; tierce in the middle of the morning; sext at noon; none in the early afternoon; vespers before supper; and then compline, the night prayer. When monks were absent from sext and confessed it at culpa, they were always careful to enunciate the *t*—"For having missed sext once." In most American Benedictine monasteries today, tierce, sext, and none are replaced by one office called Day Prayer that takes place at midday. Vatican II suppressed prime.

There are some matters about which St. Benedict is insistent, and the Divine Office is one of them, although even here he allowed freedom in his time to arrange a somewhat different structure, "provided that the full complement of one hundred and fifty psalms is by all means carefully maintained every week, and that the series begins anew each Sunday at vigils" (18:23).

The prayer that was uttered in our church for respect of other kinds of piety might also have been a plea that we show honor to the diverse kinds of people with whom we pray in our own household. Our communal prayer should contribute to our sense of harmony.

Archbishop Rembert Weakland, recalling the years when he was Abbot Primate of the Benedictine Order and visited monastic houses around the world, occasionally found himself in communities where there were differences regarding

the praying of the Divine Office. He considered this a
healthy sign. The monks and nuns were concerned about a
vital issue in their lives, and they were trying to resolve the
problems of prayer.

St. Benedict has such good advice for those of us who follow
his way. He says the Divine Presence is everywhere, "but
beyond the least doubt we should believe this to be especially
true when we celebrate the divine office" (19:2). He wants us
to pray "in such a way that our minds are in harmony with
our voices." He asks us to pray "with purity of heart and tears
of compunction, not our many words" (20:3).

At a community meeting, Abbot Thomas asked us if we
really believe that the Divine Office is the monk's primary
work. Only a few monks said it wasn't theirs, but they didn't
identify the work to which they give preference. Perhaps they
didn't because they knew it would have been a losing battle.

Work

"Idleness is the enemy of the soul" (48:1). These are the first words of St. Benedict's chapter on work. He is repeating what all other monastic legislators said in previous ages. St. Jerome told his monks, "Always have some work on hand that the devil may find you busy."

I've met people who do not like their work. "It's the worst job I've ever had," a woman told me. But she had to keep it at a time when there was a scarcity of work. She couldn't afford to lose an income while looking for another occupation.

St. Benedict wants everyone to be happy in his work. He wishes for us to serve one another with love. It occurred to our abbot that not everyone who is able was washing dishes or table waiting. More of the monks now have an opportunity to "serve one another in love" (35:6).

St. Benedict is reasonable enough to understand that some monks will have to be excused from certain duties. The cellarer who is in charge of the material goods of the monastery and other monks "who are engaged in important business" (35:5) should be excused from kitchen service. This is one of the loopholes in the Rule that monks know by heart. I tried using it myself when I was the director of fund-raising for our missions, but I'm still cooking breakfast on Tuesdays.

"Let those who are not strong have help so that they may serve without distress, and let everyone receive help as the size of the community or local conditions warrant" (35:3-4). St. Benedict wants his monks to keep busy, but he does not want them to become overburdened. He knows how prone we are to grumbling, and he wants us to work under conditions where there will be no reason for grumbling.

In monastic life there was once an attitude that people should be given jobs they disliked in order to test their spirits. St. Benedict believes in testing spirits, but he says nothing about suppressing God-given talents. On the other hand, he realizes that some monks may test the community because of their talents, and he asks them to resist being "puffed up" by their skillfulness. He says such an artisan should "be removed from practicing his craft and not allowed to resume it unless, after manifesting his humility, he is so ordered by the abbot" (57:2-3).

"When can a fellow retire around here?" Abbot Alan was asked one afternoon when he was mowing the lawn and Brother Robert was laying flagstones for the patio in front of the church. The abbot pointed toward the cemetery and told Brother Robert, "The day we carry him down there."

Brother Robert had worked hard all his life. He came to the monastery at the age of fifty, after having been a successful farmer. He was a stonemason during our monastery's construction era and helped keep the building in repair afterward. He was a great reader and no doubt looked forward to spending more time with books in his old age. He never retired, however. The time for carrying him to the cemetery arrived on a March morning when he failed to show up to wash the breakfast dishes. He'd died in his room.

What does St. Benedict say about retirement? Nothing. There is no evidence of a retirement plan anywhere in the Rule. Some monks, of course, become incapacitated as they advance into old age. It's impossible for them to work.

Two of our elderly monks worked well into their eighties, practically to the days of their deaths. Brother Vital was an Austrian by birth and Father Ildephonse a German. This may explain why they wanted to work so long.

Trained as a cabinetmaker, Brother Vital had once worked for the Benedictine nuns in his native Salzburg. This was the abbey where there was a problem called Maria. "Bruder Benet, did you see the movie last night?" he shouted in the corridor the day after I'd sneaked out to *The Sound of Music*. Crippled with arthritis and unable to get around without the assistance of two canes, Brother Vital left the carpenter shop and became Father John's helper in the library.

Father Ildephonse, unable to hear or speak as the result of a stroke, worked in the library too. He could still see to read, and sometimes he practiced censorship in the library. He tossed *Portnoy's Complaint* into the wastebasket.

About work, St. Benedict says, "Brothers who are sick or weak should be given a type of work or craft that will keep them busy without overwhelming them or driving them away. The abbot must take their infirmities into account" (48:24-25). Father Odo, however, did not let a respiratory problem interfere with his task of chopping down every thistle on our property. He had an attack while out in the pasture with a college student who was spending the summer here. "What shall I do?" the young man asked. Father Odo had collapsed, and was sitting on the running board of the pickup truck. Gasping for breath, he pointed a finger at the ground and said, "Get that thistle."

The elderly are not necessarily identified here among the "sick or weak," but surely the same application of care must be extended to them. I'd like to work in the library in my declining days. I, however, am not the kind of monk who would dispose of a novel by Philip Roth.

❧ Let Me Sell You a Painting

Those who knew him learned not to become alarmed whenever Brother Lawrence had one of his "weak spells." Strangers and newly arrived candidates were often startled when we did not rush to his rescue, but his falls were carefully staged so that he wouldn't injure himself. Of course as he grew older, we wondered and worried about a genuine fall.

No doubt it was easy enough for our guests to surmise that Brother Lawrence was not always the easiest person with whom to live. He was one of those monks St. Benedict asks us to support "with the greatest patience" because of his "weaknesses of body or behavior" (72:5).

"I'm over eighty now and no abbot is going to boss me around anymore." This was Brother Lawrence's declaration of independence. By this time he had also determined that he was too old to work. He simply retired one day by staying in his room. But he didn't remain there. Retirement provided him more time for painting. He spent many hours, day and night, in his studio over the garage. I envied him. Here was a monk who was able to passionately pursue what interested him.

Brother Lawrence's passion for painting, however, became a problem. Visitors and retreatants were treated as prospective buyers. "Would you like to come up to my shop?" Sometimes he approached a guest without even inquiring. "You come up to my shop." Not everyone appreciated his paintings, which were copies from calendar art. A journalist, writing an article about the monastery and coerced into viewing the exhibit, politely described Brother Lawrence's work as "folk art."

Brother Lawrence was a raconteur who sought out audiences among the monks and visitors. Abbots warned him to clean up his act, but Brother Lawrence didn't think he ever said anything shady in his public performances. In retirement, he remained tuned to the times by watching talk shows on television. Everyone knew what he'd seen on Donahue, Sally, and Oprah. He constantly talked about the talk shows, expressing his disgust with what he'd seen and heard. One of the monks once asked Brother Lawrence if he'd also been watching the World Series.

"I'm not interested in that stuff."

Another monk observed, "He'll be glued to the tube for the Miss America Pageant, though." All his life, Brother Lawrence admired the beauty of women.

"I'm not interested in that stuff," was the baseball fan's rejoinder.

"Are you that old?" Brother Lawrence asked his junior by twenty years.

"I'm old enough to use a cane," Brother Lawrence declared one day. Then he moved on to a walker and finally a wheelchair. While he was still in the cane stage, I once saw him throw it aside and run down the corridor to give his list of art supplies to a confrere, who was leaving to go shopping in town. During a Sunday Mass, not long before his death, the infirmarian watched Brother Lawrence wheel himself out of the church at the beginning of the homily. He parked the wheelchair in the sacristy and walked to his room to smoke a cigarette.

"With the greatest patience," St. Benedict says. With Brother Lawrence we failed the patience test occasionally. Yet every monastic community needs its characters in order to practice patience. No matter what amount of screening is employed, every monastic community lets in a quota of them. St. Benedict's admonition about supporting the weaknesses of a person's body or behavior appears in Chapter 72 of the Rule, entitled Good Zeal. We must be zealous in manifesting love for the character, the eccentric, the nonconformist.

St. Benedict did not have a mold into which he could pour monks. Regardless of the differences among his followers, he asked monks to show to each other "the pure love of brothers" (72:8).

Brother Lawrence's genuine fall finally occurred in his bathroom. He was taken to the hospital with a broken hip. While he was there, cancer was diagnosed. "I have six beautiful nurses tending me," he reported when some of the monks visited him. The nurses did not always respond to his demands, however. One day he wished to be put back to bed, but the nurses insisted he remain seated in his wheelchair a while longer. Brother Lawrence overturned the wheelchair with himself in it. His request to be put back to bed was honored. Soon after this he was led to paradise in the company of beautiful angels, we presume.

The Tough Guy

The first word Father Francis spoke to me was not the least bit consoling. Seeing me on crutches when I came back from the hospital after having fallen out of the window I was washing on my first day in the monastery, he said, "Dummy!"

Although Father Francis cultivated gruffness, he endeared himself to many people. He was a born storyteller who never had to be persuaded to spin his yarns, many of them about a character named Uncle Hank. Seldom did anyone ever hear him repeat a story. His repertoire was immense.

For many years, he was our beekeeper. He knew an awful lot about bees and tended to lecture on the subject when asked the simplest question about them.

At chapter meetings, Father Francis never hesitated to voice objections or to call a spade a spade. He had a reputation for being reactionary. He was opposed to the renovation of our retreat wing and refused to enter it after the work had been completed. But when the community began holding chapter meetings in the conference room, he could no longer stay out of the retreat wing.

His sense of humor was a saving grace even when he appeared to be in opposition to majority opinion. As guest master, he quickly dispelled any notions tour groups or visitors might have had of a solemn monk. "Brother Sebastian and Brother Micah are the only two guys I know who weave all day without being drunk." That was his line when he showed people the loom in the vestment department. Another often-repeated line: "I can't take you into the cloister. Someone might be on his way to the showers, and you'd tell everyone you'd seen a monk streaking."

Father Francis was an outdoor sportsman who incubated wild fowl in the house. Turkeys, geese, ducks, and pheasants were hatched in his monastic cell. Once he raised a flock of wild turkeys that became so domesticated that they perched on our building, and some of us worried that visitors might mistake them for vultures. When the birds began roosting in the trees at night and gobbling at the first crack of dawn, the abbot said they had to leave the premises. Every evening, one of the monks would throw tennis balls at the turkeys when they stationed themselves in the trees. But they came right back and were still there to wake us much too early in the morning.

Father Francis never went to a dentist until his teeth started hurting. He went to the doctor when he had cancer. The day after surgery, Abbot Thomas called on Father Francis. "Have you got a piece of paper and a pencil?" Father Francis asked. "You'll want to write down all of my job assignments for which you'll have to find replacements."

The doctor had given him two months to live, and on the day he should have been dead, he told us he felt like calling the doctor to ask if a second opinion should be sought.

On the Friday evening a week before his death, the tower bell began tolling the customary knell whenever one of us dies, and we rushed to his room in the infirmary. Father Francis was lying on the bed, smiling. "Wrong guy," he said. Father Michael had died unexpectedly. The next time we heard the tolling bell—just as we were beginning Conventual Mass—there was no doubt of his demise and our loss of a remarkable character.

Dogs

We have never had to buy a dog. People have always given them to us. In some cases, it hasn't taken us long to figure out why. I have shown my overwhelming affection for only two of these canines, both of them purebred collies.

Katie's stability in our community was doubtful for a while. It wasn't that she was considering leaving. Abbot Denis was on the verge of expelling her. He informed four of her stalwart friends that she must either shape up or look for another place in which to reside. Katie had been with us since she was four months old. Now she was almost four years old.

We'd been excusing her behavior. Her defenders said things like, "She's only a puppy," or, "She'll change when she grows up," or, "Give her a chance." She was advancing out of puppyhood, however, and the abbot thought it was time she began showing some signs of maturity.

One of Katie's problems was not unlike that of certain monks. She had an inordinate desire to possess things. The monk who collects things can easily hoard his cache in his cell or in other rooms he has requisitioned. But Katie had to keep her loot outdoors on the east side of the monastery.

Admittedly, the yard looked messy sometimes. Well, most of the time. Katie collected pop cans, wine bottles, and plastic jugs. She stole clothing and shoes from the poor boxes. She swiped automotive parts from the garage. At Christmas time she'd run off with a camel from the nativity scene in front of the church.

Although some of the monks were disturbed by her conduct, no one in the community could overlook her ingenuity. She was able to open boxes and other containers that a less talented dog would have found impossible to get into. Twice the previous summer, she had opened cases of paper toweling for the lavatory dispensers and had distributed their contents all over the yard. Katie's critics said she was naughty, a bad dog. They didn't realize that, like everyone else in the monastery, she was a hard worker. It was no easy task, I'm sure, for her to transfer all the stacked logs for our fireplace to her side of the monastery. But she stuck with it.

Another of her problems was the exuberance with which she greeted visitors. People who came here frequently learned to tell her, "Get down, Katie. Don't jump on me." Sometimes strangers ran from her, but she pursued them. She didn't like being ignored.

When some nuns were here on retreat, one of them was praying her rosary while strolling the grounds. Sister was intent on praying, but playful Katie bit off a decade of the rosary and ran away with it. Even I thought she'd gone too far that time.

What caused the abbatial ultimatum was her ability to remove the deer-warning signals from the front bumpers of our cars. Ingenious! But they were expensive and she rendered them useless by chewing on them.

It's not that Katie was totally without scruples. She knew when she had done something wrong. Her guilt was obvious.

She had great remorse, but her compulsions were greater. Brother Mark was assigned to help her deal with these compulsions. He walked her on a leash twice a day to the scene of her crimes. If he discovered some object that should not have been located on the east side of the monastery, Katie was punished right there on the spot. This had been attempted in the past, but she had always run away, her ears back and her tail between her legs. Now she had to stay there and face up to her sins.

There were signs of progress within a short time. The yard looked neater. She was less inclined to jump on people because she was instructed to stay away from the front door. What St. Benedict said regarding monks also applied to Katie the collie. This was another case of "supporting with the greatest patience one another's weaknesses of body or behavior" (72:5).

Before Katie came to the monastery, we had a male collie. Aelred was given to us soon after he had been weaned from his mother's milk. He was not a mischievous puppy, but he was accident prone. On his third day here, he miraculously survived a fifteen-foot fall from a ramp in the garage. Shortly after that he caught his paw in a trap intended for muskrats. He had other injuries during his ten years of life, some of them the result of his clumsiness, others inflicted by the badgers he bravely fought.

Aelred liked recreating with the community, especially on nights when we had popcorn, but Abbot Alan always threw him out. Abbot Alan did not enjoy Aelred's company inside the house. One time the community convinced the prior that the abbot was away and that the dog should be invited to coffee break. Aelred could tell time. He always knew when we were at our coffee break, and he faithfully appeared at the window. Abbot Alan and the dog arrived in the community room at the same time. Naturally, the dog left first, escorted by an embarrassed prior. I was the prior.

Some people thought Abbot Alan and Aelred were enemies because the dog always barked at him and never at the rest of us. Guests often drew this fact to our attention. But there was no malice on Aelred's part whatsoever. When he was a yapping pup, Abbot Alan used to bark back at him. It was something they just carried on, a custom established between them. Monks were often able to cover their tracks because, thanks to Aelred's barking, it was easy to tell that the abbot was approaching.

Aelred could not only tell time, he could also spell. "Aelred, T-R-E-A-T?" He responded to that enthusiastically. Also: K-I-T-C-H-E-N. Once Brother Michael confused him by asking, "Aelred, want to make a R-E-T-R-E-A-T?"

Aelred woofed down whatever we gave him to eat. Katie was a finicky eater. Aelred liked riding in cars. All we had to do was rattle the key in front of his eyes and he'd bound over to where we park the monastery cars. If a visitor left a car door open, Aelred would climb in and patiently wait for the driver to return. For a long time he slept in the farm Jeep. Katie couldn't be coaxed into a car. For her there was no such thing as a joy ride. She would never willingly accompany me to Marvin or Milbank as Aelred did. In the summertime, Aelred gave his full attention to the monks who were sitting outdoors at evening recreation. Katie would join them on the benches, often crowding out a monk, but her attention was divided. If she saw a rabbit on the lawn, she'd leave us to chase it. The monks told me I shouldn't compare Katie with Aelred. This only made her feel inferior. It may even have accounted for her rebellious behavior.

The last time I coaxed Katie into a car, she went on a ride from which she never returned. We had made numerous trips to the veterinarian, but the only treatment he could recommend for her health problem was euthanasia.

One time Aelred received a post card addressed to him from Rievaulx Abbey in Yorkshire, his namesake's monastery. "Arf, arf, Aelred. It's a pretty place. The hills are luscious for romping and there are plenty of chickens to chase after, not to mention the many sheep. But you wouldn't be happy here at all, doggie. For there are no monks. And so after a while, you'd get bored sniffing and lifting a leg on twelfth-century ruins, and you'd wish you were back in South Dakota. Tell your master I said a prayer for him and all of your other friends at the monastery." St. Aelred of Rievaulx preached and wrote about friendship. And who is man's best friend? Our Aelred was certainly a good friend of mine. And so was Katie. But, oh, how I wished she could have been more like Aelred.

The Women in Our Lives

History abounds with stories of the close friendships between celibate men and women. Francis of Assisi and Clare, Francis de Sales and Jane Frances de Chantal, and Vincent de Paul and Louise de Marillac are three sets of saintly friends who come to mind. So do the uncelibate Peter Abelard and Heloise. The romance of this prominent lay theologian and his beautiful young student shocked the Parisians of their day, and the two lovers went off to end their lives in Benedictine cloisters—after Heloise's uncle had Abelard castrated.

There are saints whose relationships are bound by blood. This is especially the case with men and women who followed monastic vocations. St. Basil and his sister, St. Macrina, were the children of St. Basil the Elder and St. Emmelia. When Basil the Elder died, Macrina and her mother turned the family home into a convent. When St. Anthony of Egypt decided to become a monk, he sent his little sister, who'd been his charge, to a convent.

St. Walburga, the sister of St. Willibald and St. Wunibald, became the abbess of Heidenheim, the monastery that her brothers had founded. English by birth, they were cousins of St. Boniface, the English monk who is the Apostle of Germany. St. Lioba was another relative of Boniface's who helped him establish Christianity among the Germanic people.

When St. Bernard of Clairvaux entered the monastery, he persuaded thirty-one relatives to tag along. Among the relatives who became monks were four of his brothers. Bernard had a sister, two years younger than himself, who married a nobleman. On one of his visits to their home, Bernard scolded his sister, Humbeline, for her manner of dress and high style of living. A few years later she asked her husband's permission to enter a Benedictine monastery. Eventually, she became the abbess, succeeding her sister-in-law in that office.

Throughout history, blood brothers and sisters have become Benedictines. We've always had monks in our community who have sisters in Benedictine monasteries. We've also had blood brothers enter our community. In one year's novitiate class, two of the novices had professed brothers in the community. Besides the sibling relationship in houses of Benedictine men and women, there are sometimes other ties of kinship. A Benedictine may find himself or herself in the same community with uncles, aunts, cousins, and even a parent.

There is a familial character to Benedictine monastic life. Perhaps this is what attracts many of us to it. No doubt, with the decline in vocations, there will be fewer blood relationships in our houses, but the desire for membership in a Benedictine family is unlikely to disappear. For us, the most significant brother-sister relationship is that of St. Benedict and St. Scholastica. They saw each other only once a year, and on this particular occasion, St. Scholastica wanted to make the most of it. Brother and sister spent the whole day "singing God's praises and conversing about the spiritual life." At dusk they ate supper and continued talking at table until dark. Scholastica was so happy that she suggested, "Please do not leave me tonight, brother. Let us keep talking about the joys of heaven till morning."

St. Benedict was disturbed by this suggestion. "What are you saying, sister?" he replied. "You know I cannot stay away from the monastery." Before Benedict could leave the table, his sister prayed up a violent rainstorm. Benedict knew he was trapped there for the night. "God forgive you, sister," he said. "What have you done?"

She told him, "When I appealed to you, you would not listen to me. So I turned to my God and He heard my prayer. Leave now if you can. Leave me here and go back to your monastery."

Benedict, the lawgiver, had to bend. He had to break monastic night silence by conversing with his sister until dawn. He was already guilty of having taken a meal at a place only a short distance from the monastery. Benedict probably thought of a lot of other rules he was transgressing. Scholastica reminded him that he had intended "to set down nothing harsh, nothing burdensome" (Pro. 46), as he claimed in his Rule. She had to teach him, in this instance, that he was behaving contrary to the Rule and that love of God, and the love between brother and sister, are more important than the letter of the law.

Scholastica showed her brother, the wonder-worker, that she, too, could work a miracle. "The sky was so clear at the time, there was not a cloud in sight. At her brother's refusal, Scholastica folded her hands on the table and rested her head upon them in earnest prayer. When she looked up again, there was a sudden burst of lightning and thunder accompanied by such a downpour that Benedict and his companions were unable to set foot outside the door."

I witnessed a variation of this miracle at a gathering of Benedictine men and women during an especially hot and dry summer. A play was produced in which I had the role of Benedict, and Sister Valerie was Scholastica. She was so convincing as Benedict's sister that the audience and cast had to step over puddles and stay off the wet grass on our way to a party after the performance. Every year on the tenth of February, the Feast of St. Scholastica, Sister Valerie calls me and asks, "Brother dear, don't you want to wish me a happy day?"

On another occasion, St. Scholastica was blamed for inclement weather. Several of us were on our way to the nearby monastery of women. We'd been invited for supper, but a blizzard turned us back. It was the Feast of St. Scholastica. We supposed this was her way of letting us know that she still has control of nature's elements.

Three days after the rainstorm, St. Benedict saw the soul of his sister flying off to heaven in the form of a dove. He must have admitted to having been very foolish that night of their final meeting on earth.

Brother Gene sometimes said that he was the only member of our community who really understood women. He'd been married to one. A widower with grown children when he came to the monastery, he gave visitors a start when they heard other guests calling one of the monks "Dad" or "Grandpa."

Some of our monks have formed close friendships with women. Late in his life, Father Gregory had a widow friend of his own age. She'd been one of his tomato customers, and she kept coming back to see him even when snow covered the garden. Daisy took Father Gregory out to dinner now and then—always with the abbot's approval. Afterward, she'd ask him to accompany her to the supermarket. Seeing him properly dressed in his clerical suit and pushing the grocery cart, other shoppers might have guessed that these two old folks were a retired Episcopal vicar and his wife.

❦ The Rural Life

A monk from our neighboring monastery in North Dakota once observed that our two communities were similar: "Few monks, lots of cattle; basically blue collar." At one time, we had both a dairy and a beef herd. The milk cows were sold, and we increased the number of livestock in the feedlot. Today we have even fewer monks and no cattle.

St. Basil, the Patriarch of Monks in the East, thought that agriculture was a very suitable work for monks because "farmers are not obligated to do much traveling or running about hither and thither." Basil's monks, of course, did not have to go to town for parts when the John Deere broke down.

Abbot Thomas, in our day, also believed that agriculture was a commendable work for his monks. When we were no longer able to maintain the cattle operation, the abbot bought us some chickens and pigs. The hens provided us with eggs for about a year. Then we ate the chickens and started buying eggs again. The pigs, however, lasted a while longer.

One time when Brother Chris took three of them to town for butchering, they broke away and ran down the main street. Men with shotguns pursued them. The pigs were apprehended in front of the bank where they were shot and had their throats slit. "Watch for lead in the pork roast," Brother Chris warned us.

Although our cropland and pastures are now rented out, the monks still tend a large vegetable garden. Our orchard bears fruit from which jams and jellies are made. Bees produce honey for our table.

Brother Gene grew exquisite flowers to adorn our church and refectory. Guests were pleasantly surprised to find flowers in their rooms, and often they left with a plant from Brother Gene's greenhouse. Up until the week before his death from cancer, Brother Gene was mindful of seeing that guests had a rose in their rooms. In the summer, the patio at the entrance to the monastery was arrayed with flowers. Katie the collie spent her first summer snoozing in one of the geranium beds, another fault for which she had to be reprimanded.

St. Benedict says, "The monastery should, if possible, be so constructed that within it all necessities, such as water, mill and garden are contained, and the various crafts practiced. There will be no need for the monks to roam outside, because that is not at all good for their souls" (66:6-7). Saints Basil and Benedict both believed in giving monks enough to do, work that would keep them at home.

🌿 The Gardener

St. Benedict says, "Obedience is a blessing to be shown to all, not only to the abbot but also to one another as brothers, since we know that it is by this way of obedience that we go to God" (71:1-2). So, it was Father Gregory who sent me to the garden, not the abbot.

When Father Gregory became manager of the appeal office, I was still there typing envelopes and recording donations. Father Gregory had often complained about not having steady help in the garden. Now he was counting on me. "Things are slack in the office during the summertime," he said. "You'll be able to assist me in the garden."

I wanted to plead that I was constitutionally incapable of working outdoors. As a novice, I had volunteered on a Saturday afternoon to help load hay bales onto the farm's flatbed wagon. At suppertime my hands were so sore and swollen that I could barely hold my knife and fork. My hands were also terribly scratched because I hadn't worn gloves. On Monday morning in the appeal office, I found it painful to type addresses on the envelopes.

Housewives from three counties came here to purchase Father Gregory's tomatoes. What couldn't be sold, he gave away to local hospitals and nursing homes. Someone dubbed him "Tomato King of the Whetstone Valley." If he hadn't had this reputation to uphold, we wouldn't have had to trip over all the green tomatoes he brought into the house to ripen before the killing frost got them.

One Sunday afternoon, a man approached Frater Andrew and me at the front door. The poor man looked distraught, as if he had some heavy sin he needed to confess immediately. He asked to see a priest. Frater Andrew and I ran all through the monastery looking for a priest, but neither of us found one. I apologized to the man, who looked even more desperate. "Shucks," he said. "I wanted to buy a bushel of tomatoes."

I didn't last long in the garden. My allergist advised me to leave it immediately, saying, "That's the worst possible place for you to be working." I had been hoping this would be his response when I asked if he really thought I should be working in the garden.

Realizing the burden of age, Father Gregory encouraged younger monks to assume part of the gardening during his last two summers. By then he had found more willing and able heirs to the garden. I continued working for him in the office and eventually replaced him as appeal director. He continued the practice, though, of going on the road every autumn, after the garden had been harvested, to solicit funds from people he considered to be special benefactors. His tour took him to six states in the eastern part of the country, and he described his method for me once. "You arrive at their home late in the afternoon. After visiting with them, they usually say, 'Father, you might as well stay for supper.' After supper, I suggest we play cards. It gets to be pretty late and they'll ask me to spend the night. After breakfast, they write out a check and I tell them I'd better be on my way."

The Nurse

St. Benedict wants the sick monks to "be served by an attendant who is God-fearing, attentive, and concerned" (36:7). Brother Alex was our infirmarian when I entered the monastery. I went to his room one time for an aspirin, and I found him reading a book entitled *How to Practice Folk Medicine*. I'm sure it was in that book that he found the recipe for the throat spray he used on all of us. We swore by it—even when there was an epidemic of sore throats, and Brother Alex would spray the concoction into mouth after mouth without ever washing off the atomizer. Furthermore, there was a lot of iodine in his special remedy and none of us was ever poisoned. The miracle was that no one ever died from Brother Alex's cure.

Although Brother Alex did some things that might not have been approved by medical science, he had the proper credentials for nursing. He was a 1919 graduate of a school of nursing at a hospital in Connecticut. Brother Alex's childhood was spent in New Haven, where Teddy Roosevelt waved to him on mornings when the little boy was playing in the front yard and Roosevelt was on his way to the president's office at Yale.

Before Brother Alex came to our monastery, he was the infirmarian at our mother abbey. Our community was never large enough to require a full-time infirmarian, so Brother Alex also did our laundry. Often Brother Alex's two professions clashed. We couldn't receive much medical attention from him on Monday mornings; not even Abbot Gilbert could persuade the infirmarian to give him an allergy shot on the morning when all the dirty laundry had to be sorted and washed. The story we tell most often is about the time Brother Sebastian was helping tar the roof of the new barn. He spilled a bucket of tar all over himself and then fell from the roof. When he was brought to the laundryman-infirmarian on that Monday morning, Brother Alex yelled, "Take him out of here! I don't want that tar getting on the laundry." Lest you think St. Benedict would have fired Brother Alex for not being attentive and concerned, I hasten to assure you that he was more obliging on the rest of the days of the week—but never on a Monday.

We all remember his little peculiarities. At breakfast he always dumped a fried egg on his cereal. He was always whistling or singing, "Yes, We Have No Bananas." Once I caught him whistling his favorite tune in church while waiting for the rest of us to assemble for compline. Whenever he saw something that disgusted him, he prefaced his disapproval by saying, "Oh, for pity's sake!" He was especially annoyed when people didn't close doors. "Oh, for pity's sake, the door is open," he would mutter all the way down the corridor on his way to close the door. He enjoyed reading aloud the advertisements in magazines and newspapers and then commenting on the products he'd tested. This was sometimes a disturbance to those of us who were trying to do our own reading. Most of the time, though, we were resigned to listening to Brother Alex's commercials.

When it was decided that a younger monk should be sent away for nurse's training, Brother Alex told me, "It looks like I'm getting the boot. That Wilson boy is going to nursing school." Brother Rene was home on vacation from nursing school when Brother Gerard was hospitalized with a stroke. He and Brother Alex went to see Brother Gerard. On the way out of the hospital, Brother Alex stopped at the desk and informed the woman behind it, "I want you to know that I'm a registered nurse." He renewed his Connecticut license every year. Brother Rene returned to nursing school and Brother Gerard came home to the abbey infirmary, but Brother Alex wasn't on duty then. He was living in the infirmary too.

I became his nurse, of sorts. He had diabetes, and every morning before breakfast, I brought him his insulin. He was able to give himself the injection, but he depended on me to bring the insulin to him and to hand him the cotton swab. One summer I had two vacations because Brother Alex insisted that he needed me to accompany him on his. I'd already been to my parental home for two weeks, but Brother Alex was able to swing the deal. When several of the monks were planning a trip to one of the North Dakota missions, Brother Alex told the prior, "Brother Benet has to come along to give me my shots." Once a month he and I would go to the hospital in Milbank. He had to see the doctor early in the morning, and afterward the sister in the kitchen would give us an enormous breakfast. We both looked forward to those monthly breakfasts outside the monastery. Sometimes, after breakfast, he'd want to go downtown to the drugstore just to look at the medicines on the shelves.

Brother Rene was the infirmarian during Brother Alex's last days on earth. When I stopped by to visit the retired infirmarian one afternoon, he was reading the nine-hundred-page textbook Brother Rene had used in nursing school. It occurred to me that *How to Practice Folk Medicine* was more in keeping with Brother Alex's style.

The Missionary-Monk

Father Dan and I both arrived at the monastery in the autumn of 1958: I to begin my candidacy and Father Dan for what he called his "incarceration." He claimed the assignment to the monastery came as a punishment for the speeding fine he'd received while serving at one of our Indian missions. Within the next few weeks, I concluded that he was here for a rest. Not his own but the mission superior's. Father Dan was sometimes meddlesome and a frequent complainer. I certainly didn't get much rest on Father Dan's first night back in the monastery. His room was down the corridor from mine, and he was moving things into it until well after midnight, slamming the door every time he entered or left.

Father Dan didn't like being locked up in the monastery. He wanted to return to his ministry among the Indian people. On weekends, he was sent from here to assist in "white" parishes. He asked the congregations to pray for his release from Blue Cloud Abbey. I depended on him to mail letters for me whenever he went out on parish work, since those were the days when our correspondence was still censored.

He always abetted my crime by dropping the letters in the nearest mailbox. After three years of confinement at the monastery, he was allowed to return to a reservation. He stayed on the missions until he was called back to the monastery again at the age of eighty-eight. Although he wanted to live and die among the Indian people and be buried with them, Father Dan's resting place is in our cemetery. There was no getting away from the monastery this time.

The Indian people loved him. Those to whom he was ministering on a particular reservation sometimes protested his being assigned to another mission. Never before had so many Native American people attended the funeral of one of our former missionaries. People were here from every reservation in the Dakotas, places where our monks had never worked but where Father Dan was known. His faithful presence at the Catholic Sioux Indian Congress, held on a different reservation every summer, had earned him the title "Dan, Dan the Congressman."

He told me that in his Kentucky youth, he'd dreamed about becoming a missionary to China. The Dakotas may have seemed as distant to him as Asia when he came to these parts soon after his ordination at St. Meinrad's in 1933. Mastering the Dakota language, he edited a weekly newspaper and compiled a hymnal.

Although I was born in one Dakota and was now living in the other, I knew hardly anything about the Native people whose name the two states bore. Father Dan took me to my first powwow. Whenever I visited the mission where he was stationed, he took me around the reservation and to the homes of his parishioners. I recall getting stuck with him on a winter's drive through the woods on the Spirit Lake Reservation in North Dakota and a hair-raising ride to the top of a nearby butte on a summer's day.

In his later years, Father Dan had fewer responsibilities on the reservations, but in no way did he consider himself retired. We presumed he'd find life back at the monastery unbearable, and for this reason he was being left out there as long as possible. His adjustment to the monastery went more smoothly than any of us had ever anticipated. He pursued his interests: carpentry, photography, and swimming all year round. When our pond was frozen, he begged rides to the pool in town. He liked watching nature programs on television but often fell asleep with the remote control in his hands.

Father Dan came home to the monastery soon after an accident that earned him fame. On a windy day, while crossing the narrows on his way from the reservation, he slid off the road into Devils Lake and had to be rescued from his submerged car by a Navy SEAL, who providentially happened to be riding in the car behind Father Dan's. "I was only trying to get a closer look at the waves," Father Dan said. Three years later, in the early hours of the morning, he died of a heart attack while in our Jacuzzi.

I'd come to Blue Cloud Abbey believing that real monks didn't live outside the monastery. I credit Father Dan with being the first monk to introduce me to the reality of American Benedictinism—the reality of my own community. Although St. Benedict believed monks should pursue their prayer and work in the enclosure of the monastery, American Benedictinism has always responded to various needs of service outside the monastery.

During his last years here in the monastery, Father Dan was happy among the brethren and helpful wherever and whenever he could be. He was prompt about attending the Divine Office. St. Benedict says we should have an "eagerness for the Work of God"(58:7). Father Dan, fearful of being late for this work, sometimes ran to his choir stall. He practiced good zeal inside the monastery and out of it.

Some of the Indian people objected to Father Dan's being called back to the monastery. They had a plan for keeping him with them and were willing to look after the old missionary until the end of his days. His friends on the reservation had to learn what Father Dan already knew: A monk must obey his abbot.

Dining Out

For St. Benedict it was important that the community be together at the prayer and at meals. There was a penance for being tardy at either. If the monk continued arriving late in the refectory, his portion of wine would be taken away until he made amends.

I've heard it said that it's a rare occasion nowadays when an ordinary family can sit down together for a meal. There are so many commitments that take family members away at mealtime. On a particular night, one or more children or a parent may be eating out at a fast food place instead of at the dining room table.

St. Benedict frowned upon his monks eating out. "It was a custom of the house, strictly observed as a matter of regular discipline, that monks away on business did not take food or drink outside the monastery." The abbot, however, could give permission, and St. Benedict made an exception for himself the evening he dined out with his sister. Once a few of the monks "stopped for a meal at the home of a devout woman they knew in the neighborhood. On their return, when they presented themselves to the abbot for the usual blessing, he asked them where they had taken their meal." They lied about having done so without their abbot's permission.

Even without any crumbs on their habits or mustard on their faces, St. Benedict knew exactly what these monks had eaten and how many cups they had downed. I suppose Benedict's concern is the same a modern-day abbot would have. There are other devout women in the neighborhood who are anxious to entertain monks—maybe even some who are not so devout. Father Gregory's friend was a devout lady. Going to other people's homes too frequently, however, may foster excessive dependencies and involvements outside the monastic community.

Years ago, when Brother Gerard's cooking left a whole lot to be desired, those of us who had clinic appointments looked forward to a meal outside the monastery. If enough monks had appointments stretched throughout the afternoon, it would be suppertime when we went to the hospital to have prescriptions filled. And the sisters always invited us for supper.

Cooking was a chore for Brother Gerard, but he accepted it as an act of obedience, a means of sanctification. He was a poor planner. Meals were often late in the early days of his cooking. Our pioneers recall the undercooked chicken dinner he once served them only an hour after the chickens had still been running around in the yard.

One of the monks always said, "If Gerard would get his butt out of church and into the kitchen, we'd have supper on time." He did spend a lot of time at private prayer in the church.

Once I went to the clinic in the morning with Abbot Gilbert, Father Ildephonse, and Brother Felix. We got out at noon. "Now, we'll go to the hospital for lunch," Brother Felix informed us.

"I don't think we should," Abbot Gilbert said. "The monks are making nuisances of themselves by taking so many meals at the hospital."

"You do what you want. I'm going to the hospital."

Brother Felix was driving, so we all ate at the hospital.

In St. Benedict's biography there is another story about an unlawful meal. One of Benedict's monks, Valentinian, "had a brother who was a very devout layman. Every year he visited the abbey in order to get Benedict's blessing and see his brother. Now, one time as he was making this journey he was joined by another traveler who had brought some food along."

Although Valentinian's brother fasted on his trips to Monte Cassino, his traveling companion invited him to share a picnic lunch. Upon arriving at the monastery, St. Benedict confronted the brother. "At this, Valentinian's brother fell at Benedict's feet and admitted the weakness of his will. The thought that even from such a distance the saint had witnessed the wrong he had done filled him with shame and remorse."

The man was not a monk, but like monks he'd made a commitment to not eat between meals. "No one is to presume to eat or drink before or after the time appointed" (43:18) St. Benedict says in the Rule. He does, however, grant the superior the right to give an individual monk something between meals on occasion. The communal meal is so important to Benedict that when a monk, on his own, eats or drinks between meals, he is showing disrespect for his brothers. St. Benedict also insists that his monks arrive at meals promptly. Some of us are tardy now and then. We watch the network news and linger on to catch a bit of the local at six o'clock. The abbot has to remind us that we should arrive in the refectory on time for his blessing of the food.

John Cassian, a monk of an earlier period, was also cautious about eating between meals. He saw the monastery orchard as a great temptation. "When the fruit is hanging enticingly on the trees and not only knocks against their breast as they pass through, but is also lying on the ground and offering itself to be trampled under foot and, as it is all ready to be gathered, it would easily be able to entice those who see it, to gratify their appetite. The chance it offers and the quality of the fruit should excite even the most severe and abstemious to long for it. Still, they consider it wrong not merely to taste a single fruit but even to touch it with the hand unless it is put on the table openly for the common meal of all."

One year thieves got away with all of our apples just as they'd ripened. This robbery most likely occurred in the daytime, but none of us witnessed it. Another heist occurred at night when twenty-four cases of beer were stolen from the kitchen storeroom. The thieves partied on our lawn, and we had to gather up the empties in the morning.

Damien

Father Gerald's death was discovered when he didn't show up in the church one morning; Brother Robert's when it was observed that one of the breakfast dishwashers was missing; and Father Damien's because of his absence at a holiday cocktail party. Abbot Alan interrupted our festivity to announce a death in the community. We put down our glasses. In our state of shock, no one thought of tolling the bell for Father Damien.

He had been resting in his room all day because he had not been feeling well for several days. Some of the monks had knocked on his door throughout the day, but when he had not responded, they had presumed he was sleeping. He'd placed a Do Not Disturb sign on the door. At the age of forty-five, he had been delivered from every kind of disturbance on this earth.

We sometimes felt that Father Damien was a disturbance to us. He disturbed our complacency, our comfort. Father Damien was always thinking of something new for us to do. Often these projects became solely his because our enthusiasm was not forthcoming. We referred to "Damien's art festival" and "Damien's crowd of people." He once told me that ours was the kind of community in which the individual monk had to carve out his own career.

He studied at the Catholic University of America in Washington, D.C., and at the Pontifical Biblical Institute in Rome, where he was awarded a licentiate. We presumed he would come home and teach Scripture to our clerical students. But while he was away, the decision was made to send our clerics to other monasteries for their priesthood training.

Many of us were anxious for Father Damien to return even if he didn't have a professorship waiting for him. Some of us felt isolated from what was happening outside the cloister. Damien had been exposed to new ideas and experiences. None of us had protested against the Vietnam War, but Damien had participated in public demonstrations at the nation's capitol. The youth of this era were being referred to as "The New Breed." We needed a novice master who could understand where the kids who were entering the monastery were coming from. Damien had been out there with them.

Eyebrows were raised when he began organizing inter-novitiate workshops for the neophytes, male and female, of the religious communities in the diocese. The purpose was educational, but the participants also had a good time. Some of our older monks were shocked when they heard that Damien and his novices were dancing with the women in our church basement.

He was also in charge of the Institute for Christian Brotherhood, the name he gave to our ecumenical work. These were the days of ecumenical dialogue, and Father Damien brought numerous Protestants and Catholics, clergy and laity, to the monastery for profitable discussions and lectures. One year he brought a rabbi to us during Holy Week for a Seder service. Some of the monks complained about the long ceremony—and about having to eat a roast of lamb.

Father Damien was in demand for workshops and lectures outside the monastery, but in some quarters he was held suspect. Complaints about him were made to the abbot. He got into trouble in one convent for introducing an offertory procession. Having two of the sisters bring the offerings of bread and wine to him at the altar was not a custom approved by the local bishop, although Vatican II had introduced this liturgical practice. Father Gerald had accompanied Father Damien to that workshop, and both of them were told by the bishop to never again function as priests in his diocese. His successor let it be known that they could come back, but by then they were both dead.

When the archabbot of St. Vincent's in Pennsylvania was elected Primate of the Benedictine Order, he asked Father Damien to serve as his secretary. Although Father Damico's headquarters were in Rome, he traveled with Abbot Primate Rembert Weakland on visitations to Benedictine monasteries of men and women throughout the world. We found it providential to have a man in Rome when there was a threat that the Benedictines might have to return to a Latin liturgy. Damien cleared up matters for us at the Vatican.

After four years, he came home and resumed his directorship of the Institute for Christian Brotherhood. If he were still in that position today, I'm sure the institute's title would be more inclusive. His ecumenical work this time was centered mostly in teaching Scripture at the graduate level for two programs sponsored by Lutheran colleges in our area. He was also a guest professor at a Catholic seminary and college. In the diocese to which our monastery belongs, he was involved with continuing education for the clergy, and he taught Scripture to candidates for the permanent diaconate.

Some of us used to give Father Damien a hard time because he was away from the monastery so much. His response was that he was only following an ancient monastic tradition, one that was especially valid for our community. Our European roots are in Switzerland, and monasticism was introduced there by wandering Irish monks from Ireland. Not long after his death, on the Feast of St. Thomas Aquinas, I thought of how Damien and Aquinas were alike. Both were burned out before the age of fifty. Both had accomplished much in their short lifetimes. Perhaps, though, St. Bernard of Clairvaux is a more suitable model for Father Damien. Aquinas, after all, was a Dominican, and Bernard, like Damien, was professed to follow the Rule of St. Benedict. Bernard left his cloister often, yet he is recognized as one of the great Fathers of Monasticism.

Although he was away often, Father Damien was every bit a community man. He knew a lot about the history of monasticism, and he was aware of the direction it was going in our day because of his experience as the Primate's secretary. He didn't want us to lag behind. Just a few weeks before his death, one of us asked him, "Damien, if you were told to give up all of your work outside the monastery, would you be able to live here in peace?" He said, "Yes."

Damien and I were born in the same year, we went to the same college, and we became confreres in this monastic family. I didn't know him well in college, but in the monastery he was my brother. He was a brother to us all. We still miss his joyful presence and practical jokes. One time after a community volleyball game, Damien posted Out of Order signs on all the showers. The groans of the players resounded throughout the cloister. When they discovered this was another one of Damien's pranks, they removed every piece of furniture from his room.

Five hundred people attended his funeral. A few hours after his burial, a young man arrived here, at the recommendation of his Lutheran pastor, to discuss Scripture with Father Damien. But our Scripture scholar was gone again.

At the Movies

There was a time when we went home to visit parents and relatives every three years. This was a rather lenient policy. I'd heard of one monastery that allowed home visits only when there was a death in the monk's immediate family. In between home vacations, we went to the Black Hills every summer, where we were offered the use of a children's camp before the season opened and just after it closed. Our mode of transportation was an old yellow school bus.

Part of the community went in June and the rest in August. A creek flowed through the camp, but it was always too cold for pleasurable swimming. One summer, the people across the road let us swim in their heated pool.

We enjoyed a week of freedom from routine. Mass was celebrated daily, but we didn't have to pray the Divine Office in common. We could stay up late and in bed until the middle of the morning.

Going to the Black Hills was like visiting a foreign country. We left the prairies of eastern South Dakota and traveled four hundred miles to this mountainous and wooded region of the state. The bus conveyed us on sightseeing excursions through the Black Hills. No matter how many times we'd been to Mount Rushmore, Bethlehem Cave, Spearfish Canyon, Harney's Peak, and the graves of Calamity Jane and Wild Bill Hickok at Boot Hill in Deadwood, we always went back. But the big thrill for many of us was the once-a-year opportunity to go to the movies. We checked out the theater marquees in every town we passed through. Once we backtracked a good number of miles to see *North by Northwest*. Sometimes we went to drive-in theaters and had to park the bus sideways.

Giving up movies was the one great sacrifice I'd made in entering the monastery. The monks didn't frequent movie houses. No one ever had the audacity to ask permission to go out to a movie. There was no need for that because a movie was shown here occasionally. For a while, I was entrusted with renting the sixteen-millimeter films. Once I had to make an apology for having ordered one in which there was a scene with a naked man and woman in a bathtub—a French film.

Theater owners invited us to showings of religious movies, and viewing permission was readily granted for these. *The Nun's Story* played in Milbank the week before I made my first profession, but I couldn't attend since I was only a novice. Some years later, I saw the film on television. I was out of the novitiate when *Ben Hur* came to town.

We still don't go out to movies much. We rent or buy videos and receive them as gifts. In our part of the country, it's difficult to track down certain videos. Some of us wanted to see John Huston's version of the Flannery O'Connor novel *Wise Blood*. We could have looked in every video store in South Dakota and not have found it. In one store, the clerk told Father Guy she'd never heard of the film. "Is it an adult movie?" she asked. A friend in Milwaukee rented it for us.

One night on our way back to the camp in the Black Hills, after having attended a movie in Rapid City, someone realized we'd failed to buy milk. There would be none to pour over our cereal in the morning.

"Pull into that parking lot," Father Christopher said.

We parked the old yellow bus where he indicated, and he went into the nearby nightclub. "Could we purchase a couple quarts of milk?" Father Christopher inquired. "The grocery stores are closed now, and the wife forgot to pick up milk for the baby."

It seemed like the logical thing to say. No one would have believed him if he'd said he was with a busload of monks on their way home from a movie.

The Telephone Problem 🌿

"Answer the phone, Lum," Father Cletus says whenever he hears it ringing. He grew up listening to *Lum and Abner*, proprietors of a country general store on a popular weekly radio show in the thirties and forties.

The problem is that on weekends the phone often isn't answered. No one is on duty, and most of the monks aren't near the phone, especially on nice days in the summertime. Some monks never answer the phone because of impaired hearing or because they don't know how to connect the caller with the person being called.

Brother Felix answered our phone for thirty-five years, and in his later years it became a burden for him. Sometimes he forgot to deliver messages. His hearing was going, and this accounted for the delivery of inaccurate messages. He once gave me a call-back number for a startled stranger in South Carolina, a state in which I know absolutely no one.

He became irritated if he couldn't locate a monk who had a phone call. Before phones were installed in our rooms and places of work, Brother Felix had to come after us. "Go on the phone," he'd say. If he couldn't find the monk being called, he often expressed displeasure to the caller, who apologized for having bothered him. I answered the phone one time and the party on the other end said, "Oh! Thank God! I was praying the German wouldn't answer."

If people called after ten o'clock in the evening, Brother Felix instructed them to phone back in the morning. I overheard him tell a caller, "I not look for him now. I'm in the bed and got no clothes on."

Sometimes if a monk being called was not in the house at the moment, Brother Felix wouldn't inform the caller where he could be reached. "Don't hang up! Brother, don't hang up!" a friend of Father Stan's pleaded one time. But he did, and the man had no inkling of where to find Father Stan.

Aside from personal calls to individual monks, people phone here mostly to arrange retreats or to sell us something. The day before Christmas, callers want to know at what time Midnight Mass begins. Some of them are surprised when we tell them, "Midnight."

One time I took a call from a man who had obviously dialed the wrong number.

"Isn't this Olson's Auto Parts?"

I repeated, "This is Blue Cloud Abbey."

"What's that?"

"A Catholic monastery."

"No shit?"

"I kid you not."

I wonder what Brother Felix would have said to him.

When I entered the monastery, the phone was seldom used for anything besides business calls. We wouldn't even have entertained the thought of dialing friends or relatives just to chat. Nowadays, the use of a telephone is no longer restricted. For a while, though, the treasurer was presenting each of us with a monthly record of our personal calls. If this was intended to hint that some of us were making an excessive number of calls, it must have worked. The treasurer hasn't presented us with any telephone bills in a long time. On the other hand, he may have just given up.

Did He Really Say That?

I n speaking of the monastic life and the priesthood, I once heard Father Timothy say that God hadn't called him to either. Some of his good friends in Indianapolis were going to high school at St. Meinrad's, and he didn't want to be separated from them. So, he just followed along. When they entered the monastery, so did he. As a young monk, however, he was sent away from the Indiana monastery—even before his ordination. Since he had contracted tuberculosis, it was believed that the Dakota climate would be beneficial to him. Although he was left with only one functioning lung, Father Timothy chain-smoked cigars until a year or so before his death.

When he succeeded Father Ildephonse as the hospital and nursing home chaplain in Milbank, the smoke from Father Tim's cigars set off the fire alarm more than once, and brought the volunteer fire department to his door. While serving as chaplain, Father Tim put out a daily paper that was distributed to patients in the hospital and to residents of the home. He called it *Blab*, a fitting title for an enterprise of his.

He had a sense of humor that was at times outlandish. Community meetings were livened up by his humorous remarks, but we all knew to look for something profound beneath his apparent nonsense. Still, there were times when he was simply being silly. Answering the phone in the chaplain's quarters, he would say, "Duffy's Tavern." Once he identified himself as "Bishop Hoch here." There was a pause, and then the party on the other end said, "Father Timothy, *this* is Bishop Hoch."

One time I brought Father Tim home from a Sioux Falls hospital where he'd been a patient. He said the whole experience was like being interrogated and imprisoned by the Communists. When a nurse came into the room, Father Tim said, "Here comes another one of those Commies." I heard her tell the orderly who was going to assist him from the building, "When he collects his personal items at the desk, make sure that he counts his money. He says that he has a thousand dollars in his wallet." If that were so, why did I have to pay for our supper at Country Kitchen?

Father Tim's ancestry was solidly Irish, and he inherited the wit and wisdom of his race as well as its conviviality—and prejudice. Some English farmers, observing agricultural methods in our area, attended Mass here with Father Tim as the celebrant. He said some embarrassing things on that occasion, too.

 *Padrecito*

Father Lawrence was a convert to Catholicism. He often repeated the story about his Lutheran grandmother's introduction to Abbot Ignatius on her first visit to St. Meinrad's. She admired his pectoral cross, a symbol of abbatial authority, and asked where she might procure one like it for her grandson.

As a young man, Father Lawrence had joined an archeological expedition to the Yucatan. This experience formed his enduring love for the lands and people south of our border. He located the site for our foundation in Guatemala, and helped get it off the ground before answering a request to assist the monks of St. Meinrad's with their work in Peru. Father Lawrence spent a good number of years as the pastor of a *barrio* parish in Lima. Before either of these assignments, he had been on loan to the monks of St. Joseph's Abbey in Louisiana who staffed Guatemala's national shrine of Esquipulas.

During the construction era at Blue Cloud Abbey, Father Lawrence was in charge of the appeal office. A benefactor once told him that he had the "ability to charm the birds out of the trees." He did have a way that endeared him to people wherever he went. A woman motorist stopped one time when the car he was driving had a flat tire. He charmed her into changing it for him. He also had the ability to appear totally helpless.

After his return to this country from South America, Father Lawrence spent several summers in the Red River Valley ministering to Mexican-American migrants who labored in the sugar beet fields of North Dakota and Minnesota.

His Spanish-speaking parishioners called him "Padrecito." So did many of his monastic confreres. And there were four young men who called him "Grandpa." Unlike the children who called Brother Gene by the same title, these really weren't Father Lawrence's grandchildren. When he was in Peru, Father Lawrence befriended a family whose son he brought to this country to attend high school. Gustavo stayed here and married. Father Lawrence was very proud of Gustavo and Susan's four sons. One of them once baffled a playmate by telling him, "Our grandpa is coming to see us. He's a priest."

Father Lawrence's last assignment was chaplain for the Benedictine sisters of Mother of God Monastery in Watertown. During this time, his health began failing. One year at Christmas Midnight Mass, he fainted. An ambulance was called. While their chaplain was on the floor waiting for a ride to the hospital, the prioress suggested that the nuns sing something. She got them started on "Joy to the World."

The last year of his life, Father Lawrence was confused and sometimes he appeared not to recognize us. He remained jovial, however, to the end of his life. I stopped to see him one day, and he told me all about the dinner party he'd arranged at a fine hotel. "How was it?" I asked.

"No one came," he said.

Not long after that, he left for the heavenly banquet.

Where We Live

Several years ago, legislators in North Dakota rejected a proposal that sought to change the name of the state to Dakota. Some North Dakotans felt that the state would improve its image by dropping the North, as in "the frigid north." I've lived in both Dakotas and found that both have the same kind of weather: long cold spells in the winter—subzero temperatures made even more unbearable by the wind chill factor—and long hot spells in the summer. The temperaments of the people who live in these two states are also the same. Perhaps it would make more sense to merge the two states into one and call it Dakota, as the land was called back in the undivided days of the Dakota Territory.

The truth of the matter is that we like our separate identities, which were celebrated in 1989 when North and South Dakota observed their centennials of statehood. People from other parts of the country, however, tend to confuse us. Some of them think Lawrence Welk came from South Dakota, and others think Mount Rushmore is in North Dakota. A lot of outsiders think the Dakotas are a joke. Johnny Carson always thought Fargo, North Dakota, was especially funny.

When I checked in at an airline desk on my return to South Dakota from Albuquerque, the clerk looked at my ticket and said, "Sioux Falls, South Dakota! How awful!" I suppose many other people presume South Dakota is a terrible place to live.

In fact, a lot of Dakotans leave their states. Most of them leave for the reasons of employment and a different kind of lifestyle. The Dakotas are agricultural states, and if one isn't going to be happy down on the farm, it's better to leave. Unfortunately, in recent years many farmers have been forced to leave the land because they could no longer afford farming.

We are a prairie people living mostly on big farms and in small towns. The land is largely flat, and I suppose this is why outsiders are inclined to think of its inhabitants as flat, too. Dakotans, they might say, are dull people. But while our pleasures may be simple, we enjoy them.

Marvin is the kind of town where you could find a good part of the citizenry assembled at Wanda's Donut Shop for an afternoon coffee break. She had to close her business, however, because of poor health. There is still another place, across the street, where townspeople can socialize. But the Marvin Bar doesn't open until later in the afternoon. The bar and the post office are the only places on Main Street where business is transacted nowadays. Both of the churches—Lutheran and Baptist—were closed for a while. Another group of Lutherans has begun worshiping in the building vacated by the Evangelical Lutheran Church of America, and someone is using the Baptist Church for storage.

Marvin now has fewer than thirty residents, but hundreds of former townspeople came back for the three-day celebration of South Dakota's centenary. Many of these people had moved great distances from Marvin and South Dakota. The school they had attended had been torn down. The grocery store was gone, the blacksmith shop, the bank, and a couple of other buildings. The lumberyard was closed, and so were the café and the filling station. Some homes were gone, too, and others stood empty.

On Saturday afternoon, everyone gathered for a talent show and speeches by the old-timers who had never left Marvin. In the evening, there was a street dance. Sunday afternoon, they were back again for the parade. All the other little towns around here also had Centennial Parades in which the same floats, the same antique farm machinery, and the same horses appeared. But no matter how often we've seen them, a parade on the plains is a wonderful thing.

An ecumenical worship service was held in our church on Sunday morning. The Marvin celebration ended on Monday, when two wagon trains, which were traveling throughout South Dakota during the centennial year, came to town. On them arrived Father Odilo and Brother Rene, who had gone over to Twin Brooks to board a wagon for a ride back to Marvin. It took them three hours to travel six miles. The forty-five wagons passed through the monastery grounds, and the monks followed them into town. We all especially enjoyed the barbecue prepared by the people of Marvin.

Miracles

Deacon Peter asked Gregory if St. Benedict's miracles were worked by prayer or at the drop of his hat. Gregory told him, "Holy men can undoubtedly perform miracles in either of the ways you mentioned."

We're expected to believe that St. Benedict was not only a prophet and clairvoyant but a worker of miracles as well. He brought back to life one of his own monks and also the child of a local farmer. He cured leprosy and insanity. He cast out a devil. In times of great need, he miraculously procured a flowing spring, an overflowing barrel of oil, and pieces of gold. His prayers mended a broken tray and caused an iron blade to rise from the bottom of a lake and rejoin itself to a scythe handle. The modern reader of this biography of Benedict is inclined to regard these miracles with skepticism.

Life in Italy had been disrupted by barbarian invasions, and we've been told that Gregory wanted to comfort and encourage his native people with these stories. They point out that Italy is a land of saints, a land favored by God. The people were willing to accept miracles; they were looking for miracles.

Peter asked, "How is it that we cannot find people of this type today?"

"I believe there still are many such people in the world, Peter. One cannot conclude that there are no great saints just because no great miracles are worked. The true estimate of life, after all, lies in acts of virtue, not in the display of miracles. There are many, Peter, who without performing miracles, are not at all inferior to those who perform them."

Are we sophisticated people of this century really willing to write off miracles? I heard a television evangelist promise his viewers miracles if they would tune in to his program the following week. I've been to Lourdes, France, where I saw many people praying for miracles. I'm like Flannery O'Connor, however. When she was offered a trip to Lourdes to seek a cure for her lupus by bathing in the miraculous waters, she said, "I'd rather die for my religion than take a bath for it."

But miracles surely do occur, even in our day. Haven't all of us witnessed them? Recovery from addictions, forgiveness by people who have been abused, acceptance of the death of a loved one—all of these are kinds of miracles. Father Larry, who worked at an AIDS hospice for two years, was on hand for the deaths of twenty-seven residents, but now he knows people whose quality of life has been restored by a miracle drug.

St. Benedict, in the Prologue to his Rule, suggests how each of us may obtain a miracle. "What is not possible to us by nature, let us ask the Lord to supply by the help of His grace" (Pro. 41).

Destruction

St. Benedict is also credited with having the ability to see into the future. "One day on entering Benedict's room, [the monk Theoprobus] found him weeping bitterly. After he had waited for some time and there was still no end to the abbot's tears, he asked what was causing him such sorrow." St. Benedict responded that "Almighty God has decreed that this entire monastery and everything I have provided for the community shall fall into the hands of the barbarians. It was only with the greatest difficulty that I could prevail upon Him to spare the lives of its members.'"

This was St. Benedict's vision of the destruction of Monte Cassino by the Lombards in 589. St. Benedict was spared, however, the shedding of tears over the subsequent calamities that befell his monastery: its sacking by the Saracens in 843, the damage of an earthquake in 1349, and the bombing by the Allies in 1944.

The Lombards, like the Germans in World War II, wanted Monte Cassino for a fortress. In both cases, the advance of enemy armies could be kept under surveillance from the mountaintop. Unlike the Lombards, the Germans did not loot Monte Cassino. They assisted in transferring all the art treasures and other valuable possessions to safekeeping in Rome before the bombing. And the monks got away that time, too. Like the Lombards, the Allies destroyed Monte Cassino.

It would be edifying if we could claim that it was always a resentment of our holiness that caused the sacking of monasteries. But this is not the case. Our wealth and power and moral corruption have been reasons for the confiscation of monastic property. Monarchs and peasants alike, as well as the religious leaders of the Reformation, were pretty much fed up with the control monks had over the lives of people under the feudal system.

Even after monasteries had been reformed on the Continent and had survived the French Revolution and the Napoleonic Wars, the threat of suppression remained. The French government threw out the monks of Solesmes four times between the years 1880 and 1903. Our own mother abbey in Indiana was founded in 1854 as a refuge for monks who feared suppression by the Swiss government.

In the sixteenth century, Erasmus called monks "brainsick fools" who were "in love with themselves, and fond admirers of their own happiness." Nowadays, we receive compliments from people who have visited our monastery as guests or retreatants. We presume that we are liked. But not everyone likes monks, not even today when our image has changed considerably since Erasmus knew us. A few years ago, we had to remove our sign along U.S. Highway 12 because someone had spray painted an obscenity on it. Bullets later riddled another sign. Had St. Benedict foreseen these barbaric desecrations, he might have wept again.

On the other hand, he might tell us to weep more often for the wounds we've inflicted, for causing the bitterness that has led to such destruction.

Neighborly Acts ❀

I n the midst of a blizzard, our neighbor asked us to help him find his stray sheep. Frater Hugh strayed away from the searchers, and they had to look for him too. During dry seasons, we're called upon to help put out fires along the railroad track. Sometimes sparks from the train engine cause fires on our own property as well.

Some of the monks provided assistance in building the new post office in Marvin. The neighbors borrow tools and machines from us, and we help out whenever we can.

The daughter of one of them once called the monastery from her home in Minneapolis. Her mother and two aunts and an uncle were living on the family farm north of Marvin. Three of the siblings lived beyond their hundredth birthdays. A woman looked after them but didn't have the strength to pick them up should they ever fall. "I worry about those old people falling," she said. "If that happens, could one of the monks go over?"

The first time it happened, Brother Paul was sent to the rescue. As he helped Victoria, the woman's aunt, to her chair, she said, "The only reason I fell was so a nice young man would come along and take me in his arms."

Every summer the neighbors and monks have a picnic in our backyard. I once heard one of the neighbors tell a stranger, "You must see our abbey."

When they bought the property, the monks were struck by the neighborliness of the people from whom they bought it— despite some of the neighbors' initial misgivings about having a monastery so nearby. The abbot of our mother abbey in Indiana, after informing the owners of his interest in procuring their farm, recorded in his journal: "Mrs. Kasperson invited us to eat breakfast: coffee, sausage, pancakes, fried eggs, and toast. The Kaspersons are Norwegians and they impressed us favorably." Like my own Norwegian kinfolk and acquaintances, the Kaspersons didn't allow anyone to leave their house hungry. Years later, Cora Kasperson brought relatives to see Blue Cloud Abbey. I offered them coffee in our refectory. Cora remarked, "I used to pitch hay right on this spot."

Olena Ramsey lived in Marvin from infancy to old age. Her husband, Emil, ran the poultry produce store in town. After his death, she continued to live in Marvin until she had to go to a nursing home in Milbank. "Olena, do you recognize me?" I asked when I saw her in the corridor, sitting in a wheelchair. "I'm Brother Benet from the abbey." She smiled and said, "Well, aren't you going to kiss me?"

I did the neighborly thing. I told this story in the Marvin Baptist Church on the Sunday afternoon on which some of us attended the congregation's last service. Olena had belonged to the church all her life. Wanda of the Donut Shop remarked that she wouldn't mind if I kissed her some time. I used to deliver the evening paper to her, and now and then she'd give me a bag of doughnuts. I seldom arrived back home with a full bag.

The closing of the church was a bittersweet ceremony. Only a few people were left in the congregation, and they, like the Lutherans, would now have to find another place to worship. Former parishioners were present that day to reminisce about pastors and Sunday school teachers and events that had taken place in the church. Some of them shed tears. When the history of the congregation was read, gratitude was expressed to the monks for having given the Marvin Baptist Church an electric organ some years earlier, the organ that was used right up until the end.

Protestants and Poets

While this monastery was being built, we often asked ourselves what we would do with it when the construction era came to an end. What work could occupy the monks living here while their confreres were engaged in the ministry on the Indian reservations and at our young monastic foundation in Guatemala? (Our monastery building hadn't even been completed, and we'd established a daughter house in Central America.) Apart from the work of celebrating the liturgy, which is common to all monasteries, was there a particular apostolate that could be fostered here? The answer came with a decrease in novices and clerical students in the 1970s. The space formerly utilized by them was turned into facilities for retreatants and other groups.

It soon became known that Blue Cloud Abbey was a place where people could assemble. The rooms provided for these people were small monastic cells with plywood walls. When Brother Paddy was shown to his quarters upon arriving at the monastery to begin his candidacy, he said, "This is a fine closet. Now show me my room." Although there were few objections by retreatants to these Spartan accommodations, it was becoming apparent that a renovation of the retreat wing was needed. The electrical wiring and plumbing had to be replaced. A major reconstruction of the wing, which was over thirty years old, occurred in 1984.

Now the retreat center has twenty-one rooms with double occupancy and private baths, a conference room, a kitchenette, a lounge, and an audio/visual room. Groups wishing to use this facility are advised to book a year in advance. The greater number of retreat groups are affiliated with religious denominations, but educational institutions and public service organizations also use the facility.

St. Benedict wished for all people who come to a monastery "to be welcomed as Christ" (53:1). He said, "Proper honor must be shown to all, especially to those who share our faith and to pilgrims" (53:2). St. Benedict did not draw up an exclusive guest list. He simply said *all* people are welcome. He did not discriminate against anyone or any segment of society.

No doubt so many Protestants are drawn to a Benedictine monastery because its ancient traditions predate the conflicts that led to the Reformation. There are numerous sects within Christianity today, but, as in St. Benedict's time, they share a common faith in the person of Christ. Whatever doctrinal differences exist are of no consequence in extending hospitality. The following list of church groups that came here in a single month indicates the ecumenical dimensions of our monastery: clergy of the Episcopal Diocese of South Dakota, diaconal candidates of the same diocese, a men's organization of the Reformed Church, a marriage enrichment program of the International Four-Square Gospel Church, and intern pastors of the Evangelical Lutheran Church of America.

Catholics, of course, come here, too. Marriage Encounter, Engaged Encounter, and the Knights of Columbus, as well as priests and deacons of the Sioux Falls Diocese have all made retreats at the monastery. Parish confirmation classes and the Daughters of Isabella have come for days of recollection.

Catholics and Protestants are invited to join us in praying the Divine Office. An Episcopalian who prays with us often says, "It's so easy to enter into the flow of prayer, so quiet and slow as though you mean each word." Some of the monks think we should pray faster and not have such long pauses between psalms.

Individuals come on their own to make retreats, and we've built two winterized hermitages near our lower pond for retreatants who wish a greater degree of solitude. Another facility on the monastery grounds is Camp Mahpiyato, which operates all summer in a wooded ravine beyond the pasture. Various youth and adult groups book its use.

Under the auspices of our retreat center, a literary festival was held at the monastery in the autumn. The several regional poets and writers who initiated the event faithfully returned annually for ten years to read their work. They and other literary people still find refuge here to pursue writing now and then, free from the disturbances in their normal environments.

Brother Gene, the grower of roses, wrote poetry and read it at the festivals. A month before death claimed him, he read, in a weakened voice, one of his poems that the festival participants had printed as a broadside—their farewell gift to him.

I also read at the festival. At one time I had a modest success in having fiction published in literary journals. Once when one of my stories was read in the refectory, I heard one monk say to another monk, "That was pretty interesting stuff even if it was fiction."

Sometimes I ask visiting poets to read for the community, but I'm often fearful that no one will show up. Poetry is not a high priority for most of the monks. One year at the festival, I announced to the audience at the Saturday evening readings, "No sense waiting for any of the monks." The World Series had just begun, and I knew they'd dashed off to the television room immediately after the Divine Office let out.

Kathleen Norris remembers a young monk who appreciated the poetry reading she held for us one evening. A junior who'd come to the end of his temporary commitment, he departed from monastic life the next morning on the motorcycle he'd been hiding down the road at a friend's house for the past four years.

Ah Sure, That's What You Are

You can't fool the Irish. At least I couldn't. Unlike my confrere who pretended he was an insurance salesman, I had no intention of concealing my identity when I went to Ireland on a sabbatical, but neither did I intend to traipse everywhere around the country in monastic garb. I was above board with Lilly Connolly from Belfast when my brother and I met her in the tearoom at Bunratty Folk College near Limerick.

She was having tea at the table next to ours, and joined us when she heard our American accents. She liked Yanks.

I introduced myself. "He's a Benedictine monk," she yelled to her companions, other lady pensioners on an outing in the Republic. "Maybe he'll hear your confessions."

Everyone in the tearoom heard Lilly. They smiled at me. I told her that I couldn't hear confessions. "I'm not ordained to the priesthood."

No bother. She had a good story to tell about confession. Her sister told the priest that it had been six weeks since her last one. After listening to her for a while, the priest interrupted and said, "If you don't hurry up with this confession, it's going to be another six weeks before you finish."

And there was the story about her nephew's baptism. His mother, still in hospital, had Lilly take the wee thing to the church. Her sister had insisted that the baby was to be christened Ciaran—the Irish spelling with a *C* and not a *K*. "I told the priest. He poured the water, and said the words in Latin, of course, back then. Looking at me, he says, 'I baptized it Ciaran with a C.'"

My brother wanted to take her picture. Lilly was obliging, but she had to find her teeth. Searching through her purse, she muttered, "Where are you?" Finding them at last, she ducked her head beneath the table, and popped the dentures into her mouth. "Will you stand alongside?" she asked me. I did, and afterwards, she hugged and kissed me. She liked Yanks. She remembered all the American soldiers who were stationed in Northern Ireland during World War II. Many of them had been made welcome at the Connolly's home. "Aye, they were good lads."

By myself in Mrs. Kelly's souvenir shop in Cashel, having coffee and a scone while waiting for the bus to Holy Cross Abbey, a medieval Cistercian monastery that has been restored, herself asked me, "Have you seen a lot of Ireland?"

I told her my brother and I had come over together and toured for three weeks before he went back to the States. We'd gone by Bus Eireann. "Renting a car would have been too expensive," I said.

"Go on with you, priests have gobs of money," she replied.

I wasn't certain that I had heard her correctly. "Did you say priest?"

"Isn't that what you are?"

"I'm a brother."

Our conversation ended when some teenage girls, wearing the uniform of their school, came into the shop to buy candy.

The bus arrived. I took the seat directly behind the driver. A few miles out of Cashel, he stopped to speak with a farm-woman who appeared at the side of the bus. "Sorry, Maureen, I forgot again on this run."

She cursed. It was not four o'clock in the afternoon, and she hadn't had a cigarette since early morning.

When she cursed once more, he told her, "Don't be talking like that. There's a priest on the bus."

"Wrong," I informed him. "I'm a brother."

"I knew you were something," he said.

Although I continued to travel through Ireland in civvies, the Irish people persisted in identifying me as a man of the cloth. I went to the Duty Free Shop at Shannon before boarding the plane for home. The shop had not opened. I had only a short time before my flight would be announced. A man who appeared to be an airport employee passed by me, saying, "It'll open in a few minutes, Father."

Only once did someone get it right. A woman greeted me with "Good evening, Brother." But, of course, I was standing in front of the Christian Brothers' School in Thurles, County Tipperary. When I kissed the Blarney Stone, the man assisting me said, "You smacked it just like a priest."

Seeking and Finding

"Bernard, why have you come here?" This is the question
St. Bernard of Clairvaux asked himself every day of his
novitiate. No doubt he repeated the question often
after he'd become a busy abbot, a zealous monastic reformer,
a prolific writer, and a popular preacher.

In the rituals of entrance and profession, we are asked,
"What do you seek?" We respond, "The mercy of God and
fellowship in this community." What is it that St. Benedict
asks of anyone who enters the monastery? He wants to know
if we truly seek God. In the novitiate and even in years later,
the monk sometimes asks, "Can God be better sought in
some other place?" For a few monks, there is valid enough
reason for their going elsewhere in search of God.

St. Benedict says the novice "should be clearly told all the
hardships and difficulties that will lead to God" (58:8).
Benedict certainly experienced enough obstacles in his own
search. In the beginning, he had to overcome lustful temptations. He had to face two attempts of assassination: one by his
monks; the other by a neighbor. There were accidents in the
construction of his monastery at Monte Cassino. He had to

put up with clumsy, careless monks; monks who disobeyed; monks who lied. But he persevered. He was patient.

There are many support groups in our day, and most everyone is entitled to membership in one or the other. St. Benedict's Rule is about the support we owe each other as a Christian community. St. Benedict encourages the practice of patience.

I suspect some people may grow impatient with us because we do not always appear in the vanguard. Benedictines are old-fashioned people. Cardinal Newman seemed to understand us: "St. Benedict found the world, physical and social, in ruins, and his mission was to restore it in the way not of science, but of nature, not as if setting about to do it, not professing to do it by any set time, or by any rare specific, or by any series of strokes, but so quietly, patiently, gradually, that often till the work was done, it was not known to be doing."

Abbot Thomas once asked this question of us: "What does being a monk mean to you?" Being a monk has provided me with a home. The monastery is the only home I've had as an adult. I came to it as a twenty-one-year-old innocent from a small town, right out of college. A young man with whom I'm acquainted was told by the monks of a monastery he tried joining: "Go around the block a couple more times, and then come back to us." When I entered the monastery, I hadn't even been around the block once. There are other Benedictine houses that are more famous than mine, better known for their works, their architecture, their culture, and various other admirable qualities. But I'm not at home in them. I'm here. This is where I've grown up.

It is obvious from reading St. Benedict's Rule that he intended to establish a home. He saw the monastery as a place where the inhabitants would usually be at home. There is a father in this home and he is responsible for his household. A good part of the Rule is concerned with its practical management. We all profess stability in this monastic family. Benedictines are the only religious order in the Roman Catholic Church who profess a vow of stability in a particular community. The monastery is like an old family homestead. It's where we're born into this way of life and nurtured in it. The monastery is the place to which we always return. Eventually, we die here and are buried among our family members.

We've all come to the monastery from families where particular customs prevailed. St. Benedict requires a certain amount of common observance in his family and expects us to develop attitudes that conform to his. Yet he recognizes the individuality of every member of his family. It is tragic when families have irreconcilable differences, when someone who differs from the rest cannot be respected or loved.

St. Benedict tells us to stay at home. He assures us that we're always welcome in his kind of home. He speaks a language of love and respect for the people who dwell in his house, and he asks them to communicate in a like manner. "To their fellow monks they show the pure love of brothers . . ." (72:8).

When I was visiting with someone from the outside to whom I expressed several of my disappointments and frustrations, he asked, "Why do you even stay in the monastery?" The answer is simple: I know I'm loved here. Regardless of my prejudices and eccentricities and differences and failings, I'm still loved. I'm with the right support group.

Bernard of Clairvaux belonged to a relatively young monastic order, which had been founded for the purpose of restoring the authentic practice of St. Benedict's Rule. The Cistercian founders had broken off from the Benedictines so that they might "keep the Rule and their vows."

In my younger years, I sometimes asked myself, "Should I transfer to the Cistercians?" Not Bernard's Cistercians, but the reformed branch, the Trappists. Regardless of the imposed hardships, their life seemed more idyllic than mine. Unlike the monks in our kind of community, Trappists were not distracted by a call to the missions. I was convinced their much simpler way of life placed a greater value on the essentials of monasticism than ours ever would. Now that I'm older and have a greater sense of stability in my own monastic family, I never suffer that kind of temptation. But the whole ambiance of strictly enclosed Trappist life was once an attraction. Even the image of a white-cowled monk holding a Trappist fruitcake fascinated me. I'd overdosed on Thomas Merton.

Right Where We Belong

I n the days of Totila, there was a Goth named Zalla—a
terrorist. "No monk or cleric who fell into his hands ever
escaped alive," Gregory claimed. Zalla terrorized a
farmer, trying to make him cough up money. In order to
get him to stop beating him, the farmer said all of his
money was with Benedict. Zalla bound the farmer's hand
with a rope, and told him to lead the way to the Abbot of
Monte Cassino.

When they arrived there, St.Benedict was reading. It was
time for *lectio divina*. "The brothers should have specified
periods for manual labor as well as for prayerful reading"
(48:1). Zalla ordered Benedict to go fetch the farmer's
money. The abbot looked at the farmer's bound hands, and
the rope immediately came untied. "Benedict called for his
monks and had them take Zalla inside for some food and
drink." After being urged to change his behavior, "Zalla
went away thoroughly humbled and made no more demands
on the farmer who had been freed from his bonds by the
mere glance from the man of God."

One day when another farmer came to Monte Cassino
carrying the dead body of his son, Benedict was just coming

in from the fields. "They must not become distressed if local conditions or their poverty should force them to do the harvesting themselves" (48:7).

The farmer pleaded with Benedict to restore the boy to life. Benedict protested that "the holy apostles are the only ones who can raise the dead." The boy's father would not give up. Benedict prayed over the body. The boy came back to life. "Benedict then took the little boy by the hand and gave him back to his father alive and well."

St. Benedict was where he should be and was doing what was supposed to be done at those times. It was time for *lectio*—Zalla came upon him reading. It was time for coming in from work—the farmer found him returning from the fields.

We Benedictines have our schedules. I came across Stella Pretty Sounding Flute and Agnes Grey sitting in the lobby one morning. Stella said, "Here we are. We've got an appointment with Abbot Alan, and just like white people we're on time."

We Benedictines have our routines. Human beings need routine. Someone who has a ministry among street people has pointed out that they too keep to routine: walking the same streets daily, looking into the same dumpsters, sleeping in the same places. In doing this, they are retaining a basic relationship with people and places.

St. Benedict, in the Prologue to his Rule, says: "The Lord waits for us daily to translate into action, as we should, his teaching" (35). Following a daily routine is certainly a key concept of the Rule and Benedictine life. The reality of our life is that we live day in and day out right where we are, whether that is inside the monastery or working away from it in a parish, chaplaincy, or mission. Cardinal Hume, himself a monk, called everyday Benedictine spirituality "the sacrament of the humdrum."

Whatever is scheduled should be done promptly. Get out of bed right away, Benedict tells us. Carry out the superior's wish promptly. Satisfactions for mistakes at common prayer must be made right then and there. An apology for other mistakes must be made at once before the abbot and community. As soon as guests arrive, the abbot and monks are to welcome them.

There are things we have to do every day and we are expected to do them on schedule. "While there is still time," Benedict says, "while we are in this body and have time to accomplish all these things by the light of life—we must run and do now what will profit us forever" (Pro. 43-44).

🌱 The Road We Take

St. Gregory claimed that St. Benedict was aware of his approaching death. "Six days before he died, he gave orders for his tomb to be opened." On the day of his death, two monks had a revelation in which they saw a road "covered with rich carpeting and glittering with thousands of lights." This was the road from the monastery to heaven. An angel appeared to the monks and asked, "Do you know who passed this way?"

"No," they replied.

"This," he told them, "is the road taken by blessed Benedict, the Lord's beloved, when he went to heaven."

Those of us who follow this same path will assuredly reach our destination. Although we may encounter some bumps and potholes along the way, the last stretch is bound to be smooth. Benedict tells us in the Prologue of the Rule, "Do not be daunted immediately by fear and run away from the road that leads to salvation. It is bound to be narrow at the outset. But as we progress in this way of life and in faith, we shall run on the path of God's commandments, our hearts overflowing with the inexpressible delight of love" (48-49).

St. Benedict and the generations of monks and nuns after him have left us a good road map. We know where we are going. Cardinal Newman said, "To the monk, heaven was next door; he formed no plans, he had no cares; the ravens of his father Benedict were ever at his side. He went forth in his youth to his work and to his labor until the evening of his life; if he lived a day longer, he did a day's work more; whether he lived many or few, he labored on to the end of them. He had no wish to see further in advance of his journey than where he was to make his next stage. He ploughed and sowed, he prayed, he meditated, he studied, he wrote, he taught, and then he died and went to heaven."

Now, in the evening of my life, I continue on the same road I've been traveling for over forty years. I expect I'll stay on this road until it comes to an end. Like the monk's life described by Newman, mine is dedicated to routine.

Garrison Keillor wakes me every weekday morning at six with *The Writers' Almanac*. After showering and putting on my habit, I go downstairs for a cup of coffee before Lauds. I wave at Father Gus as I pass through the refectory on my way to the kitchen. He's there every morning having coffee and meditating on the liturgical readings for the day. Lauds begins at a quarter to seven and lasts twenty minutes. There is a quiet period before breakfast at seven-thirty. We eat breakfast in silence except on Sundays and feast days. Work begins at eight o'clock. Most of my work time is devoted to answering mail from our Oblates of St. Benedict, men and women who apply the teachings of St. Benedict to their lives in the secular world. I also have the responsibility of assigning certain weekly duties in the monastery: the dishwashers, table waiter, table reader, master of ceremony, and cantor.

At ten-thirty, we do reading in our rooms for an hour before day prayer and Mass. Lunch is afterward, and work resumes at one o'clock. I take the outgoing mail into Marvin at three and come back for the fifteen-minute communal coffee break. Work ends at four-thirty, and vespers begins at five. Supper is at six o'clock, followed by another hour of *lectio* and then the office of readings, after which we recreate by watching TV, playing cards, or conversing. Most of the monks retire to their rooms by nine o'clock.

St. Benedict urges us to do all these things also with good zeal because it "leads to God and everlasting life" (72:2).

The Last Benedictine Pastor of Devils Lake

F ather Gerald taught for several years in the high schools we administered on the Indian reservations. In 1970, he became the superior of St. Michael's Mission in North Dakota on the Spirit Lake Reservation. That was the same year we began transferring the schools to the ownership and operation of the local tribes. Father Gerald was the first mission superior to accomplish this. Although he liked working on the reservation, he spent the last years of his priestly life in the nearby town of Devils Lake as the pastor of a "white parish."

Although Father Gerald sometimes liked to pretend that he had a gruff personality, he was really a cheerful person with a fine sense of humor. He was a dedicated missionary, teacher, and pastor who did not hesitate to take on additional responsibilities in whatever assignments he was given. Although he was the only monk of his generation in our community who used snuff, Father Gerald had a penchant for neatness and cleanliness. He was orderly about everything.

Preferring to work away from the monastery, he liked to feign symptoms of illness whenever he returned to it. Seeing the bell tower after making the bend in the road from Marvin, Father Gerald claimed that he always felt weak and his body began to ache. We knew this was another ruse. Once here, he was healthy enough to play handball. Often he stayed an extra day in order to play a couple more games of handball.

Father Gerald had as much fervor for dancing as he did for playing handball. Because of his state in life, he was unable to dance as often as he liked. He belonged to the Elk's Club, and was sometimes spotted dancing there. Once a confrere and I, visiting Devils Lake, were invited to dinner with him at the home of parishioners. After the meal, he danced with the hostess. I was humiliated on that occasion, not by his dancing, but because I spilled the gravy bowl on her fine linen tablecloth. Perhaps St. Benedict was reluctant to allow monks the privilege of dining outside the monastery because of our boorish manners.

In 1976, Father Gerald was named one of the five most influential people in Devils Lake—population 7,222. Although three different Benedictine communities had staffed the parish for nearly a hundred years, we had made the decision to withdraw from there. Our leaving from Devils Lake was hastened by the death of the pastor. The parishioners were waiting for him in church that weekday morning, but he didn't show up. Father Gerald had died in his sleep the evening before. His funeral was here at the abbey on the day of his fifty-fifth birthday.

The Saints in Our Cemetery

On All Soul's Day and again during our annual retreat, the community gathers around the graves of our confreres. A plot for the cemetery was designated soon after the monks arrived here. When I came to the monastery, there were very few elderly members in the community. They may have been following St. Benedict's suggestion that monks think about death daily, but my generation probably didn't pay a whole lot of attention to it. Death seemed so distant. With the first death in the community twelve years after its founding, we were stunned by the reality that the young may indeed die ahead of their seniors. Brother David was only thirty-three.

Whether we go to the cemetery together or separately, we linger at the graves, remembering the monks who were once with us above ground. I recall how sentimental Father Augustine was. He could easily be moved to tears, even when viewing Lassie on television. Yet he disliked every dog we ever had, including the collies.

Someone else may remember Brother Gerard's awful cooking as well as his Irish temper. Once, brandishing a cleaver in hand, he chased his helper out of the kitchen.

Nothing ever seemed to disturb Father Casimir. The son of Polish immigrant parents, he even laughed at the ethnic jokes told about his people. For a while, Father Casimir made the coffins in which we bury our dead. He was buried in the last one he built.

Moving from gravestone to gravestone, we find ourselves quoting the monks buried beneath them: Father Michael's advice to novices, "Never let the novice master think he's in charge"; Brother Martin's counsel to newcomers assigned to work on the construction of the monastery, "Just carry a ladder all day long and they'll think you're working"; and Father Brendan's adamant "Piffle" as he concluded an argument which could have lasted up to an hour.

The date of death on Father Cuthbert's stone is December 24, 1972. We remember his death occurred while he was watching a football game on television. A slip of paper had fallen out of a book he'd had with him. Written on it in his hand was: *Today is the day.* We wondered if this referred to the Feast of Christ's birth or to our confrere's death.

Brother Gene's remains were not interred until a couple years after his death. He had requested that his body be donated to the University of South Dakota Medical School with the proviso that his ashes were to be returned for burial in our cemetery. Until that happened, Brother Francis used to tell people that Brother Gene had gone to college. One day I heard him and Brother Chris figuring out how many credit hours Brother Gene should have earned by then.

We remember the circumstances of our confrere's deaths. Father Gualbert died playing golf on a Sunday afternoon. Father Xavier died on his way to a movie, Father Guy in a car just after he'd come from the clinic and was on his way for a bite to eat, Father Wilfrid at a community social in the recreation room. Sitting at a table with three other monks, he suddenly fell from his chair and onto the floor. Father Stan received an honorary degree from a college the week before he had a stroke that affected his brain. He died a month later, thinking, on his less coherent days, that he was living in Alaska.

After the burial prior to his own, Father Paul told Brother Francis, on their way up from the cemetery to the monastery, "Some of us might just as well have stayed there." A visitor once asked Father Paul what his projection was for our monastery's future. He replied, "Funerals. Lots of funerals."

When I came to the monastery, I thought Frater Paul was an old man. Of course, he was older than most of us who were entering in those days. He'd been in World War II when we were still in grade school. Not yet ordained to the priesthood, Frater Paul had come to the monastery only a few years before me. He was gaunt and had an ashen complexion. A true ascetic, I surmised. He conveyed the image of a man who didn't have a funny bone in his body. As with many first impressions, this one was wrong. His wit was once likened to Jonathan Swift's. This was after Father Paul had written a satirical piece about a monastic community in which every monk wanted his own car.

Politically, Father Paul and I were on the same track, and we had mutual concerns regarding the church. Our reading tastes were also similar. Practically every time I checked out a book from the library, his name was on the card. In a recollection of his arrival at the monastery, he wrote, "I am of that generation of Americans nourished on economic depression and weaned on war. I came with a trunk full of books, among them works of the Existentialists. This made me somewhat suspect, but my interest was with them because they wrote of the concrete and they touched me where I bled." I never asked him, but I presume some of his books, like mine, must have found their way into the devil's closet.

Father Paul, had he lived longer, would no doubt have become one of our great eccentrics. In the last year of his life, following a stroke, he seemed to let go of certain conventionalities. For one thing, he stopped going to church. The abbot convinced him that he should at least attend Mass and not have Brother Rene bring communion to him in the television room. Father Paul had always been curt and we could tolerate this among ourselves, but it became an embarrassment for us when he began inquiring of visitors to the monastery, "Who the hell are you?" Someone asked me, "Has his personality changed since the stroke?" I answered, "No, it's only become more pronounced."

On the day a candidate entered the monastery, Father Paul met him pushing a cart down the second-floor corridor. Looking at the luggage and boxes on the cart, he asked the young man, "Who the hell are you?"

"I'm Michael Peterson. I've come to join the monastery."

"Be careful," Father Paul advised.

Father Paul thought some of our monastic practices were merely romantic, and he was quick to label certain ideas and proposals as nothing but "a bunch of pious bull."

Although he had the reputation of being a curmudgeon, he was not devoid of tender feelings and sentiments. He enjoyed poetry and even wrote it at one period in his life. He often quoted Rilke, his favorite poet. In a conference delivered to the community, Father Paul shed tears as he spoke of the death of his brother Bill.

Abbot St. Odo of Cluny envisaged a grand Benedictine reunion in heaven at which St. Benedict will joyfully dance with his sons and daughters. Father Paul prepared for this dance while here on earth. Whenever we sang an especially lilting hymn at the Divine Office or Mass, he swayed from side to side in his choir stall.

 *At Home*

On the day I left home to enter the monastery, we had barely left the town in which I'd been raised when one of my suitcases fell from the luggage rack on top of my brother's car and tumbled into a ditch. The thought occurred to me that maybe this was a sign that I shouldn't be going to a monastery.

On my way to the doctor after having fallen out of a window on my first day in the monastery, I asked myself if perhaps this wasn't another indication that I really didn't belong here. When I came back from a three-day stay in the hospital, I decided to give the monastery a try for at least one full month. Besides, I couldn't go anywhere with a cast on my foot.

Shortly after my accident, Brother Sebastian, my fellow candidate for monastic life, cut the tips off three of his fingers while slicing meat in the kitchen. This is the same Sebastian who fell from the barn roof and later fell off of the farm flatbed as it was making a turn. I'm sure the community must have had doubts about either of us surviving in the monastery.

Not everyone who comes to a monastery feels at home. In some cases, it takes only a few weeks to discern that one's expectations of monastic life are unrealistic, unattainable. For some monks, this discovery is not made until after several years have passed. Monastic life becomes either crushing or vapid. In either case, it is time to leave.

The story is told of an old monk who went to the novitiate dormitory every morning to wake the novice whose turn it was to wake the whole community. On one particular morning, the waker's bed was empty. It appeared the novice hadn't even slept in it. The old monk woke the novice in the next bed and asked him, "Where is Novice Anthony?"

"He's not here."

"I can see that. Where did he go?"

"He went back to where he came from."

"Why?"

"He didn't like it here."

"Who does? That's no reason for leaving."

But it is. It certainly is.

I have no regrets for having stayed. Occasionally, I meet people who have read the Rule of St. Benedict and have been turned off by it. Contrary to what St. Benedict says in the Prologue, they find his Rule both harsh and burdensome. "How can you keep a rule like that?" I'm asked. "St. Benedict is so strict." Although we offer them enough evidence of our modernity, they seem convinced that we aspire to live like sixth-century monks. The Rule of St. Benedict doesn't speak to such people in this age. "I couldn't possibly be a monk if all those things were expected of me." What do they mean? I wonder. Sleep in their clothes? Abstain from beefsteak? Drink only half a bottle of wine a day, as the Rule allows? We now wear pajamas to bed, and some monks sleep in the buff. Our diet is no longer meatless. St. Benedict, I will admit, was more generous with wine in his day, but, after all, he lived in Italy. We drink table wine only a few times a week.

St. Benedict asks that the Rule be read to novices three times and to the whole community often "so that none of the brothers can offer the excuse of ignorance" (66:8). Throughout the Rule, St. Benedict anticipates the kinds of mistakes monks will make. He tries to head them off.

I have made mistakes in my life, and I have remedied them by going back to what I learned from the Rule. Perhaps some of the monks think it was the abbot who made the biggest mistake by putting me in charge of the community's liquor supply. I had a drinking habit that developed into a serious problem over a period of ten years. St. Benedict says monks should "at least agree to drink moderately, and not to the point of excess" (40:6). With the key to our liquor closet I opened the door to alcoholism and went in all the way. Of course I was stealing from the community, and lying when the vodka needed replenishment. "They drank all of it at the Christmas party." I had finished it off and was into the gin already. I began attending AA meetings the same week I returned the key to the abbot. A few years later, I learned that as soon as I did that, the lock on the door to the liquor closet was changed.

St. Benedict always gives us another chance, a new beginning. He asks his followers, "Are you hastening toward your heavenly home? Then with Christ's help, keep this little rule that we have written for beginners" (72:8). Although I have been a monk for many years, I know that in so many ways I will always be a beginner.

One day, a few years ago, several of us monks went into town to have our eyes examined. An elderly woman was in the waiting room ahead of us and was obviously curious about the six men who had something in common besides their need for corrective lenses. She was eavesdropping on our conversation.

Her appointment preceded mine. When my turn came to see the doctor, he was chuckling. The woman, somewhat alarmed, had told him, "Doctor, those men out there belong to some kind of cult."

"It was the people of that cult who saved civilization in the Dark Ages," he informed her.

Perhaps we are needed these days for the preservation of civilization. There is so much discord in society and even in the church. "Peace" is the motto of the Order of St. Benedict. Peace is what we would like to give to the world.

Very few men enter our monastery these days, and of those who do, even fewer stay. Are numbers important to Benedictines? We were once a community of eighty, in the 1960s, but since then we have watched ourselves diminish. Numbers may determine the amount of work a monastic community can do, but they need not detract from the quality of monastic life. St. Benedict seemed to think only twelve monks were necessary. When he left his original monastery at Subiaco to found Monte Cassino, he left behind twelve monasteries with twelve monks in each. A demographer has predicted that if no one makes final profession in our community within the next ten years, our membership will be reduced to twelve monks by the end of the decade. There is no need to worry unless a community becomes so small that it is a burden to maintain a dwelling built for many monks. Should that ever happen here, we would have to move away to a smaller place, and then there would be only one tourist attraction in the vicinity: the cheese factory.

Someone who visited the ruins of Rievaulx Abbey in England told me, "What an amazing place that still is! What a magnificent monastic house it must have been!" Perhaps that's what people will say about Blue Cloud Abbey one day. Unlike St. Benedict, who had a vision of Monte Cassino's destruction by the Lombards, we just don't know the future of our abbey. A few years ago, we had a candidate for the monastery who constantly asked us and visitors, "What do you think Blue Cloud's future is?" He left here with this matter unresolved.

St. Benedict, knowing that everything he had built at Monte Cassino would fall into the hands of the barbarians only thirty years after his death, got on with the realities of present day life. He didn't brood about the future. He and his followers got on with life.

The Benedictines were not founded for the purpose of being missionaries, teachers, pastors, and social workers. We have engaged in all of these professions, but they were never the reasons for which we were founded. St. Benedict never intended to found a religious order. His Rule was written for the benefit of his own community and for any other monasteries that wished to follow it. The work to which St. Benedict gave his foremost consideration was the communal praying of the Divine Office, which he calls the work of God and to which we should prefer nothing else. This would seem to be reason enough for a Benedictine presence in our world today. This may be the reason we have survived all the great upheavals of history and why it is unlikely that we will ever go under. Individual monasteries have gone by the way, but the Order of St. Benedict has survived. We need never worry about having to abandon our primary work, the praise of God. We will never be out of work.

Monks cannot stay in church all day, however. There is other work that needs to be done in order for us to live balanced lives. The declarations of our monastic federation remind us: "The Rule of Benedict insists on work as an important part of the monk's labor of obedience. The Rule does not put work above everything else, however, or single out one type of work as more monastic than all others. Monks show their love by serving one another in whatever work they do, invoking God's blessings on tasks large and small. They share in God's continuing creation while supporting themselves by earnings and by producing for their needs."

Alcoholics Anonymous and the Rule of St. Benedict

lthough Alcoholics Anonymous is not identified with any religious denomination, a lot of AA meetings are held at churches. While visiting another monastery, one of the monks—a priest—invited me to accompany him to an AA meeting in the basement of a Baptist church. A few years before, when I was conducting a retreat at a Benedictine monastery, I went to a Monday night meeting in the basement. It was a speaker's meeting we attended at the Baptist church. The previous month the speaker had been a recovering alcoholic nun who, like the priest and me, has something else in common besides alcoholism. All three of us are members of the Order of St. Benedict. I can say no more about them. An alcoholic may break his or her own anonymity, but not anyone else's. Mine, however, was broken on my way to the very first AA meeting. I walked into a room where men and women were standing around waiting, apparently, for something to happen. The women were wearing long gingham dresses and the men had on blue jeans and western shirts. "Is this the AA meeting?" I asked.

"No," one of them replied. "It's the square dancing club."
Fortunately, I found the right room.

I attended meetings in town for several years. I still do, but
I also attend the one that is held here now on Saturday nights.
Members of AA from the surrounding area like coming to the
abbey. Patients at a nearby reservation treatment center also
attend the meetings.

When referring to the spirituality of Alcoholics
Anonymous, one quickly discovers that it has an affinity with
that of the Benedictines. In the Prologue to the Rule, St.
Benedict says, "Our life span has been lengthened by way of a
truce, that we may amend our misdeeds" (Pro. 36). For an
alcoholic, the truce is called hitting bottom. When one recognizes this, it is possible to climb back up. St. Benedict says,
"Let us get up, at long last, for the Scriptures rouse us when
they say: *It is high time for us to arise from sleep* (Rom. 13:11)"
(Pro. 8). He begins the Prologue by stating that his rule is a way
of recovery for people who have been drifting away from God
through "the sloth of disobedience" (2). An alcoholic will
confess to this same kind of behavior when taking a personal
inventory of "defects" and "wrongs."

In drawing up his rule of life, St. Benedict hopes to "set
down nothing harsh, nothing burdensome. The good of all
concerned, however, may prompt us to a little strictness in
order to amend faults and to safeguard love. Do not be
daunted immediately by fear and run away from the road that
leads to salvation" (Pro. 45–47). Although it may seem difficult at the beginning, St. Benedict predicts that one's heart
will eventually overflow "with the inexpressible delight of
love" (Pro. 49). How often one hears a recovering alcoholic
admit: "I can't begin to describe what the program has
done for me." AA promises that by faithfulness to this program, a person's "whole attitude and outlook upon life will

change." The program becomes more than a program. As with following the Rule of St. Benedict, it becomes a way of life.

AA members may also feel daunted in the beginning. "Many of us exclaimed, 'What an order! I can't go through with it.'" The AA Big Book advises the newcomer: "Do not be discouraged. No one among us has become able to maintain anything like perfect adherence to these principles. We are not saints. The point is that we are willing to grow along spiritual lines. The principles we have set down are guides to progress. We claim spiritual progress rather than spiritual perfection." This is from chapter 5, "How It Works." At the end of the Rule, St. Benedict says something similar. After telling us in seventy-two chapters how it works, he concludes: "The reason we have written this rule is that, by observing it in monasteries, we can show that we have some degree of virtue and the beginnings of monastic life" (73:1). In both the AA and Benedictine manners of living, making progress is what counts and not the achievement of perfection. Our conversion and recovery are ongoing. St. Benedict's emphasis on the day-to-day living of our monastic calling is not unlike AA's "one day at a time."

There are other parallels. "Rid your heart of all deceit" (4:24), St. Benedict tells the one who wishes to follow his way of life. AA asks new members to develop "a manner of living which demands rigorous honesty." The Prologue to the Rule: "These people fear the Lord and do not become elated over their good deeds. They judge it is the Lord's power, not their own, that brings about the good in them" (29). AA: "We admitted we were powerless over alcohol—that our lives had become unmanageable. We came to believe that a Power greater than ourselves could restore us to sanity." The Prologue: "What is not possible to us by nature, let us ask the Lord to supply by the help of his grace" (41). AA: "God is doing for us what we could not do for ourselves." The Prologue to the Rule of St. Benedict and chapter 5 of the Big Book of Alcoholics Anonymous both tell us how it works. "It works," we alcoholics say at the end of meetings, "if you work it." Once I participated in the Sunday liturgy of a community of Benedictine sisters. We held hands for the Lord's Prayer. When we let go, I almost said, as we say after the same prayer at AA meetings, "Keep coming back. It works."

The fifth of AA's Twelve Steps is this: "Admitted to God, to ourselves, and to another human being the exact nature of our wrongs." St. Benedict has twelve steps of humility, the fifth being "that a man does not conceal from his abbot any sinful thoughts entering his heart, or any wrongs committed in secret, but rather confesses them humbly" (7:44).

In chapter 40 of the Rule, St. Benedict, with "some uneasiness" addresses the subject of drinking. Admitting that he has read wine is not a suitable beverage for monks, he realizes the monks of his day can't be convinced of this. He urges them not to grumble if the amount of wine needs to be reduced or if it has to be eliminated altogether. Furthermore, abstinence has a reward for those monks who don't drink at all. So has it for members of Alcoholics Anonymous, as I have gratefully discovered.

🌿 Telling the Truth

When I was the novice master, I found myself telling the only novice during that time, "Well now, it was this way when I was a novice." When he asked permission to go after his books and other personal items that were stored in the place he'd come from, I told him, "Well now, when I was a novice all of my books were confiscated and put in the devil's closet." I assured him, though, that it was all right for a novice to keep novels in his room nowadays. I'd had to surrender my Steinbeck and Hemingway, but things had changed since then.

One of our senior monks says that it is futile to tell today's generation what it was like when we were young. There have been so many changes in the world in the past fifty years that telling young people what it was like when we were boys makes no sense. It's impossible for youth to identify with anything from our past. So many changes have occurred in the monastery since I entered it.

We thought these changes would modernize monastic life so much that there would be an influx of vocations. This didn't happen. It amazed me that a monastery in France, founded after Vatican II, had a membership of seventy and an average age of thirty-four. Novices up to the age of twenty-five were accepted. This monastery was drawing vocations because it had not accepted the changes we considered so vital. This generation had no memory of the Second Vatican Council. Just how unaware young Catholics are of that significant event was made clear when a religion teacher recently told me she'd asked her junior-high students, "What was Vatican II?" One of them answered, "The second home of the pope."

It is a mystery to me why someone who never experienced the Latin liturgy or was never acquainted with pre-Vatican II monastic observance would be attracted to it now. It is more understandable when someone of my age longs for the past. The majority of us, though, who lived through the age of monastic renovation, tend to resent the attitude that suggests that it was wrong for us to have made changes.

"Why is it that the secular world wants monasteries to remind them of the past?" an English Benedictine monk asked when he addressed a worldwide meeting of abbots. "Why does the secular world insist, rather more than monks themselves, on the importance of the imagery of the monastic habit? What is the secret of the romantic attractions of cloisters and Gregorian chant? Why are Introits and Antiphons from Silos played in traffic jams in Los Angeles?"

Are we any less Benedictines than that monastery in France? Or the one in Silos, Spain, which had a recording of chant that remained number one on the charts for months. Have we departed from both the spirit of St. Benedict and his Rule? St. Benedict was not frightened of change, of departing from tradition. He adapted monasticism for the time in which his monks were living. Although his Rule is based on traditional monastic practices, St. Benedict was himself the kind of abbot he describes in the Rule, one who ought "to be learned in divine law, so that he has a treasury of knowledge from which he can bring out what is new and what is old."

The Rule of St. Benedict has been practiced since the sixth century because it has been adaptable to time and circumstances. And it has endured because there are so many things about it that are changeless. This does not mean that monks have never had to reform their lives. There have been many monastic reform movements throughout history. The declarations of the monastic congregation to which our monastery belongs state: "The Rule of Benedict establishes a structure of monastic life. This Rule remains for succeeding ages the touchstone of authentic Benedictine life, but its principles must be applied to the present age with understanding and reflection."

Monastic historians cite the nineteenth-century revival of Benedictinism in Europe as a nostalgic restoration of the late-medieval observance rather than a genuine return to the spirit of St. Benedict. When Benedictines came to this continent in the same century, a different kind of monasticism was needed. Yet some of these pioneers wanted to cling to an Old World monastic model. When Benedictines hanker for the past, they'd better go all the way back to Benedict.

The English monk asked the world's Benedictine abbots, "Is there some way in which monks can escape from the museums in which the secular world prefers to confine them, without betraying what is essential to monastic culture?"

Some people think they will become holy simply by joining a monastery—there is an aura of holiness in a monastery that will absorb them. Another English Benedictine predicts that anyone who has entered a monastery will sooner or later "be faced with what are called negative emotions: fear, anger, frustration, boredom, hate, lust—the list is endless. It makes a monk think that he has not the necessary qualities for living monastic life; he is not a good enough person." In the words of Trappist Father Matthew Kelty in a film about Gethsemani Abbey: "There is something wrong with every one of them. Myself included." Nevertheless, he admits that he has learned to love them because they are his brothers.

Regardless of what kind of monastery a person enters today—one like ours or one like ours used to be—there are matters that need clarification from the beginning. He should be told: If you don't like people, you'll become even more annoyed by them in the monastery. You will not only have to work with people you may find disagreeable, you will have to live with them, too. You cannot walk away from them at the end of the workday.

If you've heard that monks are saints, you've been told a lie. Like everyone else, we're sinners. You may even be scandalized by some of the things that happen in the monastery.

If you are running away from yourself, you won't escape here. That's the way it is for all of us, whether monks or not: Only when we face ourselves, might we be ready to face God.

About Paraclete Press

Who We Are

Paraclete Press is an ecumenical publisher of books and recordings on Christian spirituality. Our publishing represents a full expression of Christian belief and practice—from Catholic to Evangelical, from Protestant to Orthodox.

Paraclete Press is the publishing arm of the Community of Jesus, an ecumenical monastic community in the Benedictine tradition. As such, we are uniquely positioned in the marketplace without connection to a large corporation and with informal relationships to many branches and denominations of faith.

We like it best when people buy our books from booksellers, our partners in successfully reaching as wide an audience as possible.

What We Are Doing

Books

Paraclete Press publishes books that show the richness and depth of what it means to be Christian. Although Benedictine spirituality is at the heart of all that we do, we publish books that reflect the Christian experience across many cultures, time periods, and houses of worship.

We publish books that nourish the vibrant life of the church and its people–books about spiritual practice, formation, history, ideas, and customs.

We have several different series of books within Paraclete Press, including the bestselling Living Library series of modernized classic texts; *A Voice from the Monastery*—giving voice to men and women monastics about what it means to live a spiritual life today; award winning literary faith fiction; and books that explore Judaism and Islam and discover how these faiths inform Christian thought and practice.

Recordings

From Gregorian chant to contemporary American choral works, our music recordings celebrate the richness of sacred choral music through the centuries. Paraclete is proud to distribute the recordings of the internationally acclaimed choir Gloriæ Dei Cantores, who have been praised for their "rapt and fathomless spiritual intensity" by *American Record Guide*, and the Gloriæ Dei Cantores Schola, which specializes in the study and performance of Gregorian chant. Paraclete is also the exclusive North American distributor of the recordings of the Monastic Choir of St. Peter's Abbey in Solesmes, France, long considered to be a leading authority on Gregorian chant performance.

Learn more about us at our website:
www.paracletepress.com, or call us toll-free at
1-800-451-5006.

Also by Brother Benet Tvedten

*How to Be a Monastic
and Not Leave Your Day Job:
An Invitation to Oblate Life*

ISBN: 1-55725-449-4
119 pages
$14.95, Trade paper

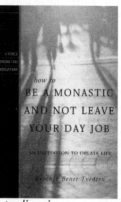

*You don't have to live in a monastery
in order to live like a monk.*

Oblates are everyday people with jobs, families, and other responsibilities. Sometimes they are Catholic, sometimes not. In today's hectic, changing world, being an oblate offers a rich spiritual connection to the stability and wisdom of an established monastic community.

"Br. Benet has long experience as a Benedictine monk
and as a wise guide for oblates, so he is extremely qualified
to write about oblates. Equally important,
he is an accomplished writer and story teller.
This book is what Benedict terms 'a tool for good work.'"
—Fr. Hugh Feiss, author,
Essential Monastic Wisdom: Writings on the Contemplative Life

"Brother Benet . . . has a delightful, dry sense of humor.
Highly recommended."
—Terrence G. Kardong, Editor, *American Benedictine Review*